Smartphone

A media revo

Smartphone Media Production

A media revolution for everyone

Robb Wallace

WWW.ROBBWALLACEMEDIA.COM

Robb Wallace Media
Glasgow
2016

Robb Wallace Media

Glasgow

www.robbwallacemedia.com

www.smartphonemediaproduction.com

Cover design : Robb Wallace

Book design : Robb Wallace

Editor : Donna Mills

First published in Scotland

by Robb Wallace Media

Printed in the UK by mixam.co.uk

ISBN

978-0-9956873-0-1

British Library Cataloging-in-Publication Data

A catalogue record for this book is available from the British library

Acknowledgements

I would like to thank first and foremost my partner Donna for all of her time, support and awesomeness. This project would not have been possible without you - you are amazing. To everyone else that helped in anyway shape or form, thank you and stay awesome :)

Book Sections

Section 1

Introduction to media production, its history and technology as well as a look at what is now possible. This section will put everything in context and inspire you to dream big.

Sections 2

An in-depth look at the smartphone's creative tools. This section includes a breakdown of core concepts for production, including how to plan, capture, edit, distribute and track your creations.

Section 3

Looks at the phone's key features for communication and distribution, delving into the key social media apps of Facebook, Twitter and YouTube.

Contents

Section 1

Section 2

Section 3

Introduction to media production, its history and technology as well as a look at what is now possible. This section will put everything in context and inspire you to dream big.

PREFACE

Who is it for? It's for anyone ready to embrace the future! Businesses, entrepreneurs, activists, organisers, authors, YouTubers, Facebookers, Twitter lovers. If you are looking to make an impact online then this is the guide that takes what you already have and shows you how to use it. Master live video, video production, photography, audio recording, social media and more.

INTRODUCTION

The future of media production is mobile. Over the last few years there has been a sharp, almost meteoric rise in the way consumers use their mobiles to access online content. The next meteoric rise will be in content creation from our mobiles. Will you be ahead of the next curve?

The trend for mobile consumption of online content will only increase due to a combination of; increasingly powerful devices, a heavily driven consumer marketplace, content creators targeting mobile specific content and finally and probably most significantly, today's youth are practically being born with a mobile device in their hand, children as young as 18 months are accessing online content via family tablets and phones.

The trend for your customers accessing your products, services, videos, websites, social media platforms etc via their mobile devices will only increase as we march into the future. However, the main focus of this book is to move from a consumer of mobile content to a creator and distributor of mobile content. This book will give you the information and the tools needed to embrace the future now and begin to utilise the fantastic technology hidden in your pocket. You will learn how to plan, capture, edit, distribute and track professional looking content, like video promos, branded photos and live streams. The ability to create marketing material from anywhere with just your phone, material that your customers will be able to access from everywhere and share with their networks and again with only their phone.

Within the content of this book you will learn how to utilise, maximise and take advantage of the powerhouse you hide in your pocket. From planning your creations to capturing them, be it video, audio and/or photographs, to editing, distributing it and finally tracking it.

I will break down the basics of content creation to show you how to create engaging video, audio, and photographs. I will point you in the direction of some of the most effective APPS available for each process, making your life a little easier by speeding up the creation process. I will also look at the accessories that will boost your productions standards. I will show you how to share and distribute your creations for maximum engagement, and finally I will show you how you can track the data to see what is working and what is not. All with just your smartphone.

HISTORY

Broadcast Technology

Broadcast technology has, for most of its life only been available to large studios with deep pockets, be it radio, TV or cinema. This is due to the high cost of equipment, the high level of technical expertise required to understand, operate and maintain the equipment, as well as the large costs associated with distribution of the produced material.

Thirty years ago the technology that we all now carry around so casually in our pockets would have been classed as a professional broadcast studio and would only have been found at the head quarters of major companies like the BBC. Just fifteen years ago, big time Hollywood producers would have cut their right arm off to get a piece of technology so comprehensive, so accessible, so portable and powerful as the device you carry in your pocket.

As digital technology progresses, the power in our pockets gets more refined and powerful. Today's mobile devices(camera and audio recorders) have the additional technology that allows them to connect with the world. Mobile phone technology like bluetooth, wifi, GPRS, and 4G allows us to access the world, to distribute our content any time and any place. No longer do you have to be a technician or a wealthy subscriber to exclusive distribution channels to broadcast your content. Anyone can simply upload to sites like Facebook and YouTube with just a click.

You already have the technology, now you just need the skills. Anyone can create a video, generally with no awareness or regard for the hundred plus years of knowledge and theory behind what makes a good engaging moving picture. Simply point or in some cases just shake and click upload. I will show you how the pros do it, I will give you solid basics in media production and all with only your trusted smartphone.

Perspective

Ten years ago, when I started editing video, I built my own home PC to deal with the intensive processes and demands of video. I built a desktop computer with 4GB of ram, a quad core processor and an independent graphics processor. That same rig, professionally built to process video, audio and photography is now matched by my high end smart phone. (2016)

Almost everyone has a media production powerhouse in their pocket. Now we must learn how to use it to drive our online life, be it sales, products, services, brand awareness etc for your business, your projects or just to highlight your passions more effectively online.

Today's world is so different from any other time in human history, technology that can enable us to become powerful content creators is progressing at such a rate, that sometimes it's hard to keep up with its development. Just have a look at the date that some of these key online services were founded! These are services that we use everyday in the connected world.

Google founded 1998
Facebook founded 2004
Youtube founded 2005
Twitter founded 2006
Whats App founded 2009
Instagram founded 2010
Snapchat founded 2011

It truly is incredible to think that services like Google, YouTube etc are so young. Google for example went from birth to the largest company in the world (now called Alphabet) in 18 years!! Technology is changing everything!! These technologies have been an integral part of life for the generation that is growing up now, and as they mature the powerhouse in their pocket will grow to take over more and more aspects of their lives. As they spend their entire lives swimming in the soup of unlimited information, the 'my phone is my world' mentality will become increasingly true, as new ways of using the smartphone develop, ways in which we could never yet imagine. Make no mistake, all future technologies will be developed with the phone at their core, it will be the hub at the centre of every great service to come.

<u>NOW</u>
The BBC (The British Broadcasting Corporation) is now actively training their broadcast teams and journalists how to use their smartphones in the journalism field. If the technology is good enough for one of the largest and most recognised broadcasters on earth, it is good enough for your business, project or group. Now, just like the staff at the BBC, you need to learn how to use it.

Hardware

The basic hardware requirements for road testing and implementing the ideas presented in this book is any modern smart phone, any mid range (and above) device that is running either Google's Android or Apple's IOS platforms.

In the first sections we will look at media creation techniques and how to implement them using the technologies offered in both Android and Apple devices. Sorry, windows devices will not be covered, the windows hardware is on par with both Android and Apple's hardware, but the apps or software available for maximising and utilising that hardware is limited by comparison. For this reason I will stick to Apple and Android. The core concepts presented don't change when applied to the Windows platform, they will even transfer to a desktop or laptop environment, however you will have to find your own apps to support the ideas presented. Please don't let that put you off because the information being presented is the key, the hardware just gives you the ability to implement it with your phone.

The below specs can be found in almost all low to mid tier smartphones available today (2016.) As media creation is based on the processing power of the computer, (ie your smartphone),the higher the spec of the smartphone, the better it will handle the workload of media creation. I recommend the below specifications as the minimum for processing video, however less powerful phones will still record audio and support photo editing and social media posting etc. At the time of writing (mid 2016), the top tier mobiles were shipping with 10 core processors, 6GBs of Ram, 128GBs of Storage and

4K cameras.

Dual core processor and above
1 Gb of ram and Above
8 Gb of storage and above
720P Movie camera and above.

The Possibilities

Your smartphone gives you the tools and technologies to plan, capture, edit, distribute and track your creations. This is your business, the world are your customers, and you know your vision better than any creative expert or freelancer ever will.

The solutions for your needs;

- For small business with limited budgets, this book will give you the means to start producing content to electrify your social media and web presence.

- For larger companies with dedicated creative staff, it will teach you how to lay down the basics of an idea - any time and place and then present that idea to your staff for them to fulfil.

- For larger business, this book can also be used as an invaluable training tool, in order to create an army of on-line content producers for your brand. Just be sure to pay them for their extra work!!

This process is not about replacing your creative staff. An expert like myself will never be replaced, well not just yet. A boss that learns a little about the creative process and better understands the technologies that are now changing the game, is a boss that will survive and a boss that will be able to communicate their creative / entrepreneurial visions clearer to their professional creative staff or freelancers. Knowing how to create content for your brand is never a bad thing. Alternatively if you are a small company, self employed and you are keeping your cost to a minimum as you push for growth, then get ready to create, with the help of this book.

The possibilities are truly endless!! Fully fledged TV commercials and even feature length films have now been filmed on the humble smartphone! Yes TV commercials and feature length films (1*). Today's businesses connect with their customers 24/7 via the various social media channels of the Internet. Major brands are continuously creating new content (live video, video, photography, audio, text) in an attempt to win new customers in this new digital battlefield. The Future is more about video than any other medium. Google, Facebook, Twitter and Snapchat are all getting ready to battle in the video and live streaming arena.

Below are some quotes from two of the leading researchers in the digital trends online space, both are clearly stating that video for business is the future.

Cisco Research (2*)
"Over half of all IP traffic will originate with non-PC devices by 2019".

"Globally, consumer Internet video traffic will be 80 percent of all consumer Internet traffic in 2019, up from   64 percent in 2014".

"64 percent of respondents indicated video content will dominate their strategies moving forward".

Nielson Research

"Generation Z and Millennials, the digital natives, are voracious consumers of media, and mobile phones are at the centre of their lives," said Megan Clarken, executive vice president, Nielsen Global Watch Product Leadership. "For younger consumers, the mobile phone is no longer just for use on the go, but everywhere — even their living rooms. Content providers and advertisers need to be flexible with their approaches in order to reach consumers where they are, on the device they are using and during the activities in which they participate."(3*)

Most of us consume content via the TV, radio and internet whilst simultaneously consuming even more content on our phone.

For example, I find my self following twitter during any major political debates to see instantly how people are reacting to each and every statement, I no longer wait for the next days papers to see how major political figures have interpreted the debate.

A large proportion of the content (text, audio, images and video) that we interact with on-line via social media was created with a smartphone, be it local news update or a professionally produced comedy sketch or a shaky shot of someone's cute dog. Our social media is full of interviews, live streams, holiday footage etc etc and a lot of it is captured and distributed via a smartphone. But media captured on the phone is also making it to main stream TV, mainly through 'citizen journalism'. From terrorism to extreme weather, celebrity appearances to local demonstrations, it all gets captured first hand on someone's smartphone. This is just one of the ways the smartphone is changing the way we consume content.

(1*)Tangerine - Feature Length - Shot on an Iphone
http://www.imdb.com/title/tt3824458/

(2*)http://www.cisco.com/c/en/us/solutions/collateral/service-provider/ip-ngn-ip-next-generation-network/white_paper_c11-481360.html

(3*)http://www.nielsen.com/uk/en/insights/news/2015/age-of-technology-generational-video-viewing-preferences-vary-by-device-and-activity.html

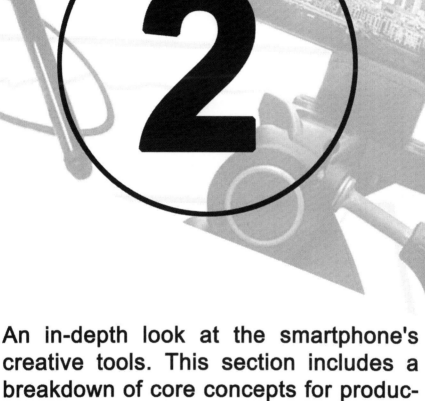

An in-depth look at the smartphone's creative tools. This section includes a breakdown of core concepts for production, including how to plan, capture, edit, distribute and track your creations.

Creating Your Brand

The backbone of your online business.

Note: All apps suggested in this book are only suggestions. For any given topic, a quick search online or in the app store will reveal many further options. Read the reviews, watch YouTube video reviews, road test different apps until you find one that works well for you.

Use your phone to keep track of your ideas. I use **Google Keep** as my main brain dump app. This is the most used app on my phone!! The No 1 used app!! It is super easy to use and instantly gives me access to creating new audio notes (Dictaphone), lists, text notes and more. Each new entry can be organised, labelled and colour coded and it is available for both Android and IOS. Solid alternatives are **Evernote** and **Awesome Note.**

Before you start creating exciting and engaging content to inspire your audience, you need to have an identity, no matter if you are a community group or a business, you will need a unique look/brand that will set you apart from the competition and be instantly recognisable and identifiable to your product or service.

If you already have an established company or group you most likely will already have a name, a logo, a tag line and some copy (copy = written materials) that describes the activities that the business or group etc engages in. If however you have not, then lets get started.

Names

Something that is related to your services – i.e My media company is called 'Robb Wallace Media'. Keep it simple and keep it relevant to the business you are in. Remember, Goggle and the other large search providers are in the business of giving their customers the best search results in relation to their search query. If there were three or four others with the name 'Robb Wallace Media,' I would have came up with another name, as I would not want google returning search results for something that was not me. (This is just a basic example of Search, however many other factors influence the order of Google search results.)

Logo

The logo should reflect your company colours and it should be clear and simple - refrain from making it too busy. For inspiration, open a new tab on your phone's browser and check out the competition, check out the market leaders in your field, as well as the largest brands in the world and then create something unique with this in mind. Before finalising it, check it against the competition and market leaders to make sure it stands up well to their branding. It really is that simple. Use the apps below to create a logo, you may even be able to make your final logo with them. At a minimum you will be able to take something to a designer and say, "I am looking for something like this", which will reduce the designers time and save you money.

Apps

- **IOS** - *LogoScopic Studio, Logo Maker, InstaLogo Logo Creator, Canva.*

- **Android** - *Logo Creator & Graphics Maker, LogoFactoryApp, Logo maker.*

- **Websites** - *logomakr.com, www.graphicsprings.com, www.designmantic.com, www.canva.com*

Colour

Being colour blind I found out really early in life that colour is a sub conscious language that most people communicate with and are influenced by, without even being aware that they are in fact being manipulated. Every culture, country, region, religion etc has different interpretations of the key colours and their meaning. Pick colours that are relevant to your market, demographic and target customer base. A quick 'Google' search will give you the emotions of each colour.

Tag Line

My media company's tag line is - "Helping business punch above their weight". Create a tag line that inspires, that fires the imagination in your prospective customers. Again, look to your competitors as well as industry leaders and international leaders. Keep it sharp and simple!!

Business description

Create two different descriptions, a short one and a long one. The short one should be concise and the longer one will give you a few more words to play with, emphasis on 'few'. Use powerful, positive and direct language to describe and inspire your potential customers about the services and products you offer. Be truthful and concise and believe that your products and services are of value. Once you have your tag line, compare it against the competition. Does it hold up or does it feel cheap and awkward?

Try this

Think of two or three brands that you readily identify with, be it a sports brand, car manufacturer or food item etc. Sum up what the brand is to you. Use single words (Adjectives). Luxurious, reliable, delicious, etc, then open a new tab on your mobile browser and see how that brand describes themselves. Your tag line and business description should be aiming to have this kind of concise dominance of its brand perception.

If you do not know what your core branding or services are then your customers will not know either. Make it very clear what you do, why you do it, when, how etc. The more you define your business, group, club etc the easier it is to describe it, to brand it.

Goal setting

Goal setting is a strong way to put your vision into perspective, a strong way for you to brainstorm, define and refine what it is you are looking to achieve. Goal setting is a fairly simple endeavour that should remain simple.

1) Write down,(use the **Google keep!** app) draw or use photographs to build an image and description of your final goal. e.g "My media company provides me and my family with a very comfortable standard of living and for this I am grateful."

For me this could be represented by a bungalow with a new car parked in the drive way.

Now break this down into smaller goals to work towards. Each smaller goal, as it is completed will be a point from where you can look back and see that you have systematically completed each of the smaller goals on the road to fulfilling your larger goal/objective. Always use positive language and talk as if it has happened and it is a certainty. The smaller goals for me for example - I built a simple, recognisable branding with a clear tag line, I created a website that brings me business, I weeded out the time consuming customers and replaced them with long term, happy, repeat customers. I now own all of the creative equipment that I use on a daily basis. etc etc.

Marketing goals. I am the name associated with mobile media production, I am actively sought out to train teams on mobile content creation. etc.

Goals should be revised and rewritten every month, use colour, pictures and firm positive language, always from the perspective that it has all ready happened.

I also like to use a three column to-do list which I then revise every two weeks. These can easily be made in **Google Docs** or **Microsoft Office Mobile**.

Todo – October 2016	Doing	Done
New Branding		x
Website SEO	x	
Social Media Updates	x	
Competitor Research		x
Customer Management and follow ups		x

Competitor Analysis

Your phone is an excellent tool for competitor analysis. Use the phone's built in browsers or just talk to your handset (ask 'Siri' for Apple devices or say 'Hello Google'for Android devices), then ask your questions.

Some key questions that everyone should ask,

1. Who are your competitors? (Long standing, most successful, what is their marketing angle?)

2. What products or services are they selling ? (How do they differ from yours? What makes yours better?)

3. How much market share do they have? (What has made them this success? Lack of competition? Great service? Superior products? Etc)

4. What marketing strategies do they employ? (local press, social media, info graphics, video, promotions, competitions,

19

loyalty schemes?)

5. How aggressive is their marketing?

6. What are their weaknesses? (marketing, products, service, value, social media, web presence)

7. Rate their threat between 1 and 10 (every few months.)

Utilise your research

Use the info you have found to help you define your audience (gender, age, interests, geography etc.) When you begin to use the **Analytics** generated by your photos, videos etc you can compare your ideal customer base vs who is actually engaging with your content and then use this information to adjust your business model.

Use all of your research to compare your initial ideas on content creation with the competition. Learn from what is working for them. Finally use their time in the marketplace to see which products work and which don't then tailor your products or services to better fit both yours and their customers.

I would recommend reading the entire book before laying down your ideas above, as the following chapters will give you lots of new ideas and new angles,from which to view the competitions strategies etc.

Customer Management

As the new customers start to engage with your content via social media, the web and email, you will have to keep track of your interactions. Keeping track of sales, enquiries, good customers, bad customers, potential customers, etc requires some sort of customer management system. This can be done via a simple spread sheet, again using **Google Docs** or **Microsoft Office Mobile** where you log each of your customers, their details, etc However, there are many dedicated mobile apps that integrate to a cloud based solution, unfortunately most of these apps incur a monthly subscription fee. Search 'Customer Relationship Management' or CRM in Google or the app store to find the best solution for you and your business.

Apps: IOS & Android
- *Zoho CRM*
- *Insightly CRM*
- *Base CRM*
- *Pipedrive*

Google Business app
The point of having a business, creating content and providing a service is to make money, for that to happen the customer must know you exist, hence your content creation.

A simple and effective way to let people know your products/ services are available is to get your business listed in Googles business directory, this will help your business websites google ranking as well!! It is a free download from the app store. Google Business and follow the simple step by step process.

Structure

You can make an equivalent looking version of anything you see on line, just with your phone. You will not be able to recreate the works of an entire department of Hollywood specialists, this is almost granted but what can be achieved is truly remarkable.

Each part in the creative sections of the book are broken down into Planning, Capturing, Editing, Distributing and Tracking. Below is a general description of each.

Planning
Planning is the key to any endeavour, taking the time to understand the why, how, where, when etc will give you a greater understanding of your ideas, and this will give your ideas greater clarity, which will lead to saved time in the long run. The planning section will give you a clear understanding of how you should be thinking with regards to that particular medium.

Capturing
Here I will describe the specifics as well as the rules for the medium, the best apps for capture, as well as additional technology that can give you the edge.

Editing
Again I will describe the specifics, as well as the rules for the medium, the best apps for editing, and tips and tricks to give you the edge.

Distributing

Here we will look at the best social media platforms, as well as the best practises to get your content working.

Tracking

How are your customers engaging with your new content? What age group, what medium, what platform etc is engaging with your content? Here we will look at some of the free tools available to track your metrics.

Why?

From here on in its all about making media, however creating new engaging content takes time, effort and imagination. So why should you take the time to create 'free' content for your customers? Why should you give up your time to learn the art of creative capture and then learn the technical skill of editing your master pieces? And then more time again to distributing it online. Here is why!

You're not just creating FREE content! You are creating marketing material, you are creating awareness, you are strengthening your brand, your sphere of influence, establishing your self as an industry expert and all of this from your pocket, anytime, anywhere.

Creativity

There is no natural talent, there is only a desire to do! If you have a desire to do, then you will quickly master the guidelines for creating stamped photos, video blogs, live streaming etc. The more you practice, the more you try, the better you become. There is no instant Spielberg!! Even Spielberg had to learn through practice.

Create Killer Content

Creating on the fly with your phone keeps your head in the game, keeps your project in your mind, keeps you focused and ready with your finger on the pulse.

More and more customers are moving towards short videos to make purchasing decisions, be it reviews or product demonstrations. Video is today's main platform for product research. Does your full line up of products or services have a video?

The reality is that at some point, your business marketing will move away from print (papers, flyers, brochures),maybe it already has and you now just need to move away from blasting your social media front with simple word based posts and progress towards a combination of audio, photos, video, live streams and words. Mixed media or cross media posts, that can all be created on your phone. When we post creative content it is a chance for our brand to be recognised and our creative work will always link back to our website, social media channels etc, with the purpose of creating new customers, retaining existing ones and converting customers of competitors. Everything that is posted is branded, indexed (tagged) and linked.

Content that you create can be used to social proof your business, i.e. testimonials from customers highlighting how awesome your product or service is, or testimonials from industry experts. Note: Don't be shy in asking your clients or training providers for testimonials and always get a photo to go with it. To be recognised as an industry expert, a testimonial with a picture is worth a hundred without a picture. A video testimonial is even better!

Everything you create is focused on your vision, on your goals for your company, or project. Your vision must be clear so it can shape the creative decisions you make while creating audio and visual content for your growing empire. Customers, old and new love value, they love info graphics, they love videos that inform them, they love images that make them laugh but more than this they love content that is made with passion!! And if you create this content, your almost guaranteed that people will identify with and share your creative work, all of which will be branded, indexed and linked and this will in turn drive traffic and new customers to your products or services. At a very minimum, it will raise your brand awareness and google ranking. Every new piece of content you create will help improve your online presence, and before long when Joe Blogs types key words into Google, those key words should start returning your content!!

24/7 Creation

Why manufacture creative ideas and put your creative notions into reality? Because this is the future, you can either embrace it or be left behind! Curb the personal Twitter/Facebook addiction and use this time to create business content. This could simply be a tweet from your business rather than a personal Facebook status update or an unrehearsed live stream of your evening at the beach to drive a particular product or service. The best creative content is in touch with the creator's emotions, it is something they are passionate about. Make it fun and the ideas will flow.

Short attention spans.

Online attention spans are short. People are used to getting what they want, quick! Make your content snappy, succinct and straight to the point. One minute Hollywood movie intros before you get to the advertised tag line just doesn't cut it online because it doesn't hold the viewers attention.

Create a Story

This is a key fundamental to any form of information sharing, like online marketing, video creation, audio information mp3s etc. We as humans love a story, from childhood to adulthood we get engrossed in a good story. From childrens' nursery rhymes that teach us cultural norms, colours, sounds etc to epic fantasy books and multi layered TV series that teach us about everything and anything. When it comes to sharing information online through a photo or video, make sure it tells a story.

The simplest formula for a story is -

- **Beginning** - Catches their attention. I.e. the problem the market is facing. A problem your target audience can relate to.

- **Middle** - Contains the detail. i.e. the inspiration that leads to the solution.

- **End** - Brings it to a close with a call to action. The solution, i.e. your product or service.

Another way to look at this could be.

Balance - disruption to the balance - regaining the balance - The end. For example let's break down the classic Arnie film 'Conan the Barbarian'.

- **Balance** - He is free living with his family.

- **Disruption to the balance** - His family is slaughtered and he is taken as a slave.

- **Regaining the balance** - Fights his way to freedom.

Moving forward, always ask your self, "What's the story?" Or, "How can I make this into a story?" A great
place to look for simple effective stories that convey key information is children's books, they are
always simple, fun, informative and fairly easy to replicate.

Apps

There are a lot of apps mentioned in this book, too many to cover the ins and outs of. I recommend that once you have decided on using a particular app, the best step forward is to launch the **YouTube** app on your phone, search the app you've downloaded and watch a few tutorials to quickly bring you up to speed on how to use the app. With this information in hand, take some time to play around with the app's features. The principles presented through the production sections will not change.

Treatment

This is the creative term used to describe the entirety of a creative project. Through each section in the book, I break down the creative projects into plan, capture, edit, distribute and track. It is a must to write out a treatment for every new project you tackle using your phone.

A treatment is as follows

Example 1

Project - Advert for new book - A short video and behind the scenes images to peak interest.

Date and Time - Filming on November 8th 2016. 8am start, to be completed for 12 noon.

Location - The Robb Wallace Media office.

Involved - Robb W, Rosie W , Jean P and Ange R

Contact numbers. Robb W 0022213212, Rosie W 35435434354, Jean P 354354354354 and Angle R 788768354678

Payment - £25 per hour

Creative outline -
A simple advert to highlight the new book by Robb Wallace. The advert will build excitement about the new book and how

it will empower readers to become creative powerhouses, all with only their trusty mobile phone. The advert will take the form of a simple interview that will see Rosie interview Robb, giving Robb the opportunity to address and sell the excellent information contained within his book. They will sit side by side and the interview will be caught in one static, locked off shot (ie a shot with no motion.) During the whole process, photos will be captured by Angela (camera shutter noise switched off)for later branding and distribution. Questions have been prepared and the full interview should not exceed 10 minutes.

Roles - Robb to be interviewed, Rosie interviewer, Jean P Camera operator, Angela R Director and photographer.

Equipment - 2 x Smartphones, 1 x external mic, 1 x powerbank or Wall charger, 1 x Camera case mount,
1 x Tripod, 1 x makeup set.

Responsible for the Equipment - Robb Wallace

Distribution – Video uploaded, indexed and tagged to both YouTube and Facebook with short teaser clips uploaded to Twitter. A blog to be created with the video, sales material and highlights of the key points. Possibly a second blog breaking down how the video was made, including the behind the scenes shots etc.

Project completion date - Aim to have it edited, uploaded and distributed for November the 12th at the latest.

Example 2

Project - Restaurant menu images.

Date and Time - 4th July 2017

Location - Big Robb's Restaurant.

Involved - Big Robb and head chef.

Contact numbers. Robb W 0022213212, Rosie W 35435434354,

Payment - Standard daily rate.

Creative outline - To create multiple images for each menu item produced that day. To then edit these images with the restaurant web address, tag line and brand for use on the website and social media channels.

Roles - Robb W will capture, edit and distribute the images. Rosie W - Head chef and producer of Awesome Foods to be captured.

Equipment - 1 x Smartphone, 1 x powerbank, 1 x Camera Flash 1 x Camera case mount, 1 x Tripod.

Responsible for the Equipment - Robb Wallace

Distribution – Blogged on the restaurant website. A

30

Facebook picture album created with the date, each image uploaded with a full description of the dish, web address, hashtags and a call to action. Individual images tweeted out with a catchy tagline and the website booking page.

Project completion date -14 July

Example 3

Project - Live video stream from Book launch.

Date and Time - August 29th 2016

Location - The Robb Wallace Media office.

Involved - Robb W and Rosie W, Jean P

Contact numbers. Robb W   0022213212, Rosie W 35435434354, Jean P 354354354354

Payment - £15 per hour

Creative outline - To live stream from the book launch to Facebook, interacting with any online users. Write a script/basic outline of what will be said.

Roles - Robb W leading the book launch, Rosie W operating the camera with onboard microphone, Jean P – interacting with the Facebook audience.

Equipment - 2 x Smartphones, 1 x external mic, 1 x Phone case with extra battery capacity.

Responsible for the Equipment - Robb Wallace

Distribution
    Before - Facebook event created to advertise the live stream one week in advance, graphics and posts informing potential viewers/participants of the event.
    During - Distribution via Facebook live.
    After – Go through all of the comments and reply personally, furthering the interactions with potential customers.

Project completion date - August 29th.

Example 4

Project - Live video stream from my travel locations

Date and Time - Anytime I am on location

Location - The world is my oys ter

Involved - Robb W

Contact numbers. N/A

Payment – N/A

Creative outline - To live stream from my travels around Europe, to gain exposure and interest in my travel blog. Interacting with any online users verbally as they join the stream or via the comments function after the broadcast has finished.

Roles - Robb W camera with external microphone and on occasion simply using the onboard microphone for convenience.

Equipment - 1 x Smartphones, 1 x external mic, 1 x Phone case with extra battery capacity 1 x Powerbank

Responsible for the Equipment - Robb Wallace

Distribution

Before - Facebook posts informing potential viewers/ participants of where and when I will be broadcasting. Asking them if they are in the area and if so come and join me live.

During - Distribution via Facebook live.

After – Go through all of the comments and reply personally, furthering the interactions with potential customers.

Project completion date - The day of the live stream.

As you can see within the treatment you are laying down everything you need to complete your project. You are clarifying your plan of action from what is being created to who's involved, what equipment is needed etc. If your treatment needs more detail, give it more but most will be even simpler than these. Send it as an **email** from your phone to all involved or if your writing them out in **Google docs** simply share it to all involved.

Audio Cheat Sheet

 Battery Charged   **Flight Mode On**

 Enough Memory   **Screen Brightness**

Plan it

Branding

External Noise

Wind Shield

Think Audio

External Mic

Describe

Audio

Good quality audio is actually the key to good quality video. If we were to compare two videos with the same average footage, one with good audio and one with bad audio, we as consumers will always prefer the video with good audio and discard/ignore the one with bad audio. The ear is the main thing we must please! Audio can be used in many ways to grab the attention of potential customers, new activist etc. The two most popular forms of audio being used to engage the end user are **Radio** and **Podcasts**. Radio is well established and features almost every style of content that can be produced from adverts, dramas, interviews and more, however it is controlled, regulated and stale. The podcast is just like a user generated radio broadcast, that is only limited by your imagination not by a studio producer or guidelines. The subject, style & format of podcasts vary greatly. They are available online via traditional podcast services like Itunes and Stitcher radio, phone apps like Beyond Pod or hosted natively via the podcasts website or with an image as a video on YouTube.

Worked Example - Gym Owner

If I were a gym owner looking to add value to the customers experience of my products and services, I would generate informative audio tracks that are accessible to the customer via the gyms website. These could include information about nutrition, recovery, hydration etc that subscribed customers could listen to at their leisure, on their commute to work etc. To grab new customers I would create FREE at home audio workouts - five minute flat tummy or five minutes to beach body etc. At the start of every audio segment/podcast would be the gym's website and an encouragement to subscribe to their social media channels, as well as any upcoming or limited membership deals.

Worked Example - Activist

If I were an activist looking to enlighten or inform the general public about the struggle a particular movement was addressing, I would use audio to inform potential supporters of the movement's ideology, history, principles etc. I would record all meetings, forums etc and post them online for transparency. I would also generate engaging interviews, concept breakdowns and regular news updates, all using the phone's simple dictaphone like features.

Planning

What is the plan for your audio? Short radio like advert? Interviews? Voice over for a video? Voice over for a photo slide show? Simple audio notes to be typed out later? Instructional for client? Podcast? These are just some of the creative ways you can use audio to push your brand, product or service.

Things to consider:

1. What is being made?
Podcast, audio for video voice over, audio for a slide show voice over, for a radio style advert, testimonial audio for your podcast, audio note etc.

2. Scriped or Freestyle?
Both have their advantages and both are suited for different

formats. Short radio adverts or voice overs for a specific product or service should definitely be scripted, using a reworking of your product copy for a precise description. On the other hand a 20 to 60 minute podcast or interview would be hard to script! In this case it would be easier to have chapters or topic cue cards to prompt you forward and keep you on track.

3. Bring the audio to life!

Audio that is not intended for video or photographic slide shows, has no visual element apart from the mind's eye of the listener. When creating an audio segment, make sure you use descriptive language to place your listener in the environment. Describe the colour, space, smell, use visual references to bring your audio to life. Another resource implemented in traditional radio is layered audio effects and foliage, this helps build up the audio world for the listener, i.e. sounds of the waves when talking about the sea etc.

4. Does quality matter?

Most audio listened to online by professional standards is low quality but to the untrained ear and the non audiophile, the standard low bit rate (low quality) MP3 will get the job done. There are many apps available to capture and output at high quality if required.

Treatment

Outline your entire treatment for the planned project and update it as your plan comes together.

Capturing

Before capturing always:

Make sure your phone is fully charged or at least has the

charge you require to fulfil the task.

Make sure that you have enough memory to record the required length of audio. 1 hour of audio @ 128KBS MP3 approx 60MB, @ 192KBS MP3 approx 87MB and @320KBS approx 144MB .

Put your phone to Flight mode so there are no incoming distractions.

Put the screens brightness up to full if recording outdoors, if the light changes you want to be able to see your screen.

Be aware of where your phones microphone is located.
Don't cover the microphones with your hands when holding the phone.

Audio is best captured/recorded in a silent area, preferably indoors in a controlled environment with no external noise. The best rooms will be carpeted and full of furniture to soak up any noise and stop it from bouncing or echoing. Unplug or remove anything that clicks, hums, buzzes etc. Major culprits are air conditioning systems, fridges, TVs and radios. Always switch all mobiles to silent as a minimum requirement but preferably to flight mode before recording so any incoming calls/texts do not break your flow or get recorded. Mobile phones that are not in flight mode can also be effected by RFI or radio frequency interference, as a note on best practice, ask everyone you are working with to put their phone on flight mode as well.

In a professional, audio recording environment, using professional equipment, there will always be the possibility to monitor the sound levels via headphones. Unfortunately, on most mobile devices there is only one 3.5mm Jack (The London Marshal has two and the Iphone 7 have none.)At a base level, using only your handset and with no additional technology, the audio levels being recorded must be monitored visually via the waveform or peak diagram on the phone's screen. However, most software designed for recording audio on smart phones are aware of this and accommodate for it, with a warning system, usually green moving into red on an indicator bar.(For colour deficient people, it is usually displayed in a visual way that makes the indicators easy to gauge without the reliance on colour recognition. If the app does not, simply download an alternative app.) The indicator will inform you if your peaking (input audio is too loud) which will result in poor distorted output audio.

When using the phone's built in microphone, keep it around four to eight inches from your face or the audio source.

If required, capture foliage or additional sounds of the environment before and or after the main audio is recorded, or create the desired audio effects later when you have time. I.e. sounds of a busy kitchen, foot steps, etc.

After recording, always listen to your segment and determine if you need to re record the segment. After a while you will master your radio voice and begin to nail your content first time, every time.

Radio voice
No one is born with a radio voice, it must be manufactured and this new voice will get better with practice. For starters, if you have a thick accent or you speak quickly, take some time to slow it down, to pronounce your words etc. I podcast from Scotland but my audience is 80% based in the USA. Due to this, I actively pronounce words that would naturally be cut short in regional dialect. My accent can be thick, so in general I slow down my speech. There is no point having excellent audio content if no one from outside of your city can understand it.

Count in
Count in to your recording, this informs everyone involved when the actual recording is live. i.e. 5,4,3, then   silence for the next two counts and you are off.

Monitor
Keep an active eye on the volume indicator on the screen to make sure your recording levels are not too loud. Also monitor the voice levels and make sure they don't go from whispering to shouting and back again. Ideally you want to keep the volume fairly equal throughout the entire recording.

Branding
Either add an indent (pre-recorded audio brand) like "www.

smartphonemediaproduction.com, the only book you will ever need" in the edit(best option) or start each audio recording with a clear introduction to your brand i.e. "This audio is brought to you by Robb Wallace Media dot com". This will start your audio recording off with your identity.

Title

Introduce yourself, the title and topic i.e. " Welcome, this episode is called 5 minutes to success with me Robb Wallace. In this episode we will be covering A, B and C"

Sharing

Encourage your audience to share your recordings. Encourage them with a simple, "If you have enjoyed this episode then please share it with your Facebook and Twitter friends, our website has lots more interesting articles and information over at smartphonemediaproduction.com. Please check it out". Always encourage your audience to share,and if you've provided a quality product or service then a percentage will be happy to share.

Subscribe

Encourage your audience to subscribe, "LIKE" or "Follow" your social media pages so they don't miss another awesome audio production.

Apps

Both IOS and Android have a native app for recording audio, both are acceptable. There are a number of professional styled audio recording apps that allow you greater editing capabilities, like adding effects, as well as features for producing your audio to a higher level (i.e. more tools for refining every aspect of the audio.)

IOS

- *Voice Memos - Simple native app that comes with IOS*
- *Garage band - A bigger app with more options*
- *I rig Recorder - Free app giving basic recording functionality with in house purchases for editing capabilities.*
- *SoundCloud - Allows you to record and upload straight to the social media sight direct from the app.*
- *Hokusai – Fully featured multitrack audio editor.*

Android

- *Audio Evolution - Professional level audio app, multiple tracks, edits, effects and more.*
- *Voice Pro - HQ Audio Editor*
- *Smart Voice Recorder*
- *SoundCloud - Allows you to record and upload straight to the social media sight directly from the app.*
- *Hi-Q MP3 Voice Recorder -Simple recorder that outputs straight to MP3. MP3 is the best audio format for 'importing audio' into Video editing apps such as Adobe Premier*

Next level solutions

A list of next level solutions are available on the website.
http://smartphonemediaproduction.com/next-level-solutions/

1. External microphones

Audio is about the microphone. Top manufacturers are creating external microphones specifically for the smart phone market and there are now some excellent options available. External microphones are better at everything. Companies like Zoom, Tascam, Fostex, Belkin, Rode and

Irig have multiple options available to meet the specifics of your audio needs, from lapel mics (small usually used for interviews), to shotgun mics (which are long and used to focus in on a sound in a loud environment) to general microphones. Whether you are using the headsets built in mic (usually on the cable of the headphones that comes with every new phone) or an upgraded external microphone, always try to use a wind shield or windscreen (fur or foam microphone cover) to dampen and reduce excess and unwanted noise produced by wind, breathing and traffic. Using a branded wind shield is a good way to brand your production physically for things like catching audio at a press conference etc, external microphones with wind shields will also improve audio capture in any environment when a controlled environment is not available.

2. Splitter
Splitters take your single 3.5mm input and splits it down into two, giving you the option to plug both a microphone and headphones into your single device. This allows audio monitoring in real time, which is always the best solution. Some external microphone solutions offer this feature as part of the microphones design.

3. Wind sock, Windshield, Windscreen for your phone
The classic foam, more associated with external microphones can be bought and slipped directly over the phones chassis, adding an instant layer of noise control to your audio recordings.

4. Earphone headset
All smartphones come with an external microphone in the box! Your phone's earphone headset comes with a built in microphone, which can be hooked up like a lapel microphone.

43

Editing

Whether you are editing your recorded tracks for a voice over video or photo slide show or as a direct radio style advert or infomercial, there are lots of apps to help you get it done. Most editing features are reserved for stand alone editing apps, most of these features will not be available in the out of the box IOS or Android app.

Importing

Most dedicated apps allow you to natively record the audio you are about to edit but if you have other audio (music, voice over, radio jingles, a sting, etc) already downloaded, edited or captured via another app or previous session, you can import that audio into your current app and add it to the project for editing. This is usually under 'Add Audio'.

Layers

Audio can overlay each other and interact with each other in layers. For example a track with 3 audio layers .

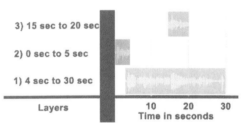

1)The top layer for example could have a woman talking about her product or service for 26 seconds, this track starts at 4 seconds and ends at 30 seconds and is the main audio layer.

2) At the beginning for 5 seconds on a separate layer (layer 2) the brand intro plays, overlaying the first layer for 1 second as it fades in to layer 1 . This track plays from 0 seconds to 5 seconds. 3) On a third layer, an audio track of an audience clapping is imported. It is set to overlap and overlay (play at the same time at a lower volume) the main audio (layer 1) at

the 15 second mark for a further 5 seconds to give the illusion that the live audience is agreeing with the claims of the sales pitch. This track plays from 15 seconds to 20 seconds. These audio layers when exported or saved will be compressed into one layer, i.e. they will become one audio file.

Editing

Is the process of manipulating the audio to get the output that you require. Editing can be as simple or as complex as you wish it to be. Start with the tracks you need to complete the task. For example, a simple radio indent would need the audio for the advert, a backing track and finally your business details or audio sting at the end (a separate pre-recorded audio sting can be imported into every new audio track created.) The video sting at the end may in itself be made of more than three layers and would be made first, saved and exported out to be re imported in as one file, one layer.

Simple radio style advert

Import the intro sting, import the main body of audio.
Add the sting to the beginning of the time line (e.g. first 8 seconds), then add the main body of the audio after it i.e. from 8 seconds onwards. Trim any count in, or excess from the beginning and end of the recording and export.

Creating your sting

The 'sting' is a short audio clip that introduces your brand, product or service. You will need to layer voice audio, a jingle and possibly some sound FX (noises). These tracks would then be arranged over the time line, with each track having an independent audio level adjusted for purpose. This would then be saved and exported out as a whole or single audio file to be used for all future audio you produce - like a short audio brand/logo for your business.

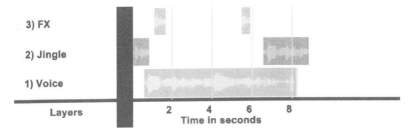

This STING would then be brought in (imported) and added to the audio (voice recording) and music (background) for the advert (or what ever you are making). Each of the three tracks would appear on their own layer. Dragging them backwards and forwards to the correct timing (location on the time line) for your purpose, trimming any excess from your audio or music tracks and snapping the sting to the beginning or end of your track. This would then be exported as a WAV file or MP3 file. Most apps also allow you to add filters to your audio, changing the pitch, speed, adding reverb as well as normalising the audio and boosting audio b` levels with gain. Just remember when playing with audio in the editing app that 1)people spend their entire lives mastering audio, you are never going to master it in a day but you will get the basics pretty fast. 2) Have fun, enjoy learning new thingsand the time will fly. Before you know it, you will be mixing promos on the train to work.

Exporting
Is the process of combining the various layers and audio clips together into one track that can be played out on any audio playing device, like your phone, mp3 player, website, video etc. When exporting your audio you will, depending on the

app, be given the opportunity to select the output quality, this determines the final quality of the audio that you will have available for uploading to your distribution platforms. The main audio export file formats are MP3, WAV and AAC. Most apps will have a standard export or save setting which will save the audio at the standard bit rate(quality) for CD standard audio. Exporting into MP3 file format is the safest export as almost every platform,phone, pc, online etc can work with them.

Distributing

During your research you may have seen some competitors using audio or came across audio ideas that have captured your attention. What platforms where they on? How were they labelled? How were they marketed?

If you have a website with server space, you can host your audio there, ask your web provider about how to upload audio to your site.

The main free hosting and distribution platforms for audio are Soundcloud, YouTube and Facebook. All of these require an account which you can do via your phone's browser or by downloading their app and setting it up. You can also upload directly to the platform via their app. The major difference between Soundcloud and both YouTube and Facebook is that with Soundcloud you are just uploading the audio then adding a thumbnail or cover art to it, the audio will play out like any other audio track, however there is limited free functionality and for more space you need to pay for a subscription. To get round this and get near unlimited hosting for you audio tracks, adverts etc you can simply convert them into videos and then host them directly on Youtube or Facebook. This technique simply requires using your created audio as the sound track to a video, the video is one single image over the duration of the audio, (making video will be covered in the video section). SoundCloud and YouTube audio can be shared through your Facebook if required. To import into Adobe Premier Clip or any other video editing app make sure the audio file is in MP3 format.

When uploading make sure you have a clear title that is equal parts catchy and descriptive. Make sure you have a good description of what is featured in the audio or what the audio is about or what it's purpose is. Use hastags #(explained later) and always label it with your web address as well as a call to action like 'subscribe', 'like' and 'share'.

Tracking

The social media channels all have excellent statistics for you to monitor. If hosting it on your website, you have many options, my favourite being Google Analytics. Look to the key information that you have determined as your demographic and use the stats to see if it is indeed being received by the correct demographic. Also use the information revealed to tailor future audio recordings to specific groups. This is covered more in the Facebook section.

Photo Cheat Sheet

 Battery Charged   **Flight Mode On**

 Enough Memory   **Screen Brightness**

Steady   **Portraite**   **Landscape**   **Thirds**

Shutter

20/80   **80/20**   **Left to Right**   **Fast 1/1000**

Apeture

F1.8   **F8**   **F32**

Medium 1/60

Large   **Medium**   **Small**   **Slow 1/4**

 49

Photography

The cameras on today's mobile phones are exceptional and to the untrained eye, it is hard to differentiate images shot on a phone from those shot on a compact or DSLR (professional) camera. The software, the lens and the sensor found in the big manufacturer's mid tier handsets and above are ample for all forms of online and basic print photography i.e. all of your marketing needs. Photographs have entire social media communities built around them, they are easy to share, they are easy to brand and they are easy to tag. In this section we will cover the basic rules and ideas of photography, planning the image(s),capturing and editing images, as well as adding your logo/brand, adding filters, tagging and distributing.

Worked Example

A restaurant owner - Phtography/Image orientated example.

Below I will outlay some of my ideas of how I would utilise the smartphone to build a buzz around a restaurant. This is only one example of almost limitless possibilities for the pocket powerhouse.

Plan, Capture, Edit, Distribute, Track

Planning
Vibrant images that highlight the quality products and services provided by the restaurant. At least two new images captured, edited, stamped with the web URL and logo, uploaded, tagged, #tagged with description each day.

Treatment

Outline your entire treatment for the planned project and update it as your plan comes together.

Capturing

I would work with the chef to make sure they were capturing fresh images of the kitchen's daily creations or daily specials, as well as the restaurant's best sellers, straight from the kitchen. These images would be about celebrating the technical ability of our chief, the high quality and artistry of the food on offer. The food photography would be standardised -i.e. a repeatable formula, a similar distance, light, angle. Then this simple standard could be learned by any member of the team to replicate the style. Other images of importance would be real customers enjoying the food, happy staff members working, smiling, clean kitchen areas, clean tables, clean interior and exterior. I would also include wider angled images(candid) of the chefs, waiting staff and bar staff at work, crafting their creations and delivering food to happy customers.

Editing

I would create a transparent image with the restaurants brand

and web address,(created using a graphics/photo editing app.) This would then be used as a 'stamp' in an editing app. Every image would have the restaurant's brand and contact details stamped upon it before being distributed on-line.

Distributing

Instagram, Twitter, Facebook and Flickr are all good social

media resources for images. I would select, at the most two of these platforms to post your photos to daily. For this example I will use Facebook. My first action would be to give my key staff members "editor status" on the restaurant's Facebook business Page (explained in the Facebook section). This allows staff to complete the process and upload images to the account. I would have my key info written, stored in a notepad app like Google keep, to allow the information to be easily accessed, copied and pasted to the status for simplicity, standardisation and speed. The information would include #tags, web address key words and a call to action (i.e. Like|Share|Comment). Each image would be uploaded with a catchy title, a short description, with some sort of encouragement to try the product and or share the post. e.g.

"Our ribs are HOT!! How hot can you go?? Come in and see if you can handle the hottest, most flavourful ribs in Glasgow!! Like|Share|Comment #hot #ribs #glasgow bigrobbs.co.uk"

Tracking
Each of the major Social media channels have a tracking/ analytics function. Facebook insights allows you to see which

demographics are engaging, how many are engaging, locations, time of day, gender, age etc. I would target the uploads via the scheduler (Scheduler is explained in the Facebook section) to meet the key times when the channel is busy as indicated by the analytics.

Planning

A photograph can convey a thousand words. Professional photographs are used in almost all major adverts, glossy magazines, product billboards etc. These images will be in most cases, intricately planned out. Someone, somewhere has taken the time to outline every detail within these images. Major brands invest a lot of time and money creating a uniformity, a colour profile, a "feel" and many more details for their marketing images.

You must do the same for your images if you want to create images that will grab your customers, that will induce those who see them to share them. For this, planning will be required. You don't have to spend five hours listing every last detail, just a few minutes to think through what you envision your customers will want and the results you want to achieve.

Your plan should start with the story you want your images to convey. In the restaurant example, the idea behind the images is to show quality food, served by happy workers to satisfied customers, in a clean environment. Look to the competition for inspiration, look to the market leaders and to the biggest companies in the world to see how they portray ideas, services and products via an image. If you start with an idea, you will have more chance of conveying it to your customers.

The best images tell a story, use powerful emotions,

exaggerated facial or body expressions and movement, use association, use symbols. It is true ' A picture is worth a thousand words', so use it to your advantage.

Things to consider!

What is being made?
The end game, what will you do with the images? Images with text overlays to advertise services, products, upcoming events, customer testimonials, events you are at, ideas you have, exclusive offers, competitions or simply a nice image posted daily will keep your brand, product and services in the minds eye of your customers.

Plan it out it or go freestyle?
The decision is yours! Once you have sat and thought about what it is exactly that you are looking to capture, once you have the overall theme of what you want to achieve, you can create a framework from which you can begin to free style. For bigger projects I would always recommend a plan, there is nothing worse than looking back and thinking, "Ah,I should have...." Planning will limit this regret.

Example: After road testing images of the chiefs creations, the restaurant manager sees a dramatic spike in engagement on his social media page. The customers love the images, they tag them and share them and as a result bookings have increased. He realises the value of good food images and commits to setting aside a small area of the kitchen, with a miniature background screen in a well lit area, where his staff can capture high quality images with the same formula and consistent settings each time. He also realises that he must leave enough room at the bottom of the picture to add his branding and contact details to each image in the editing app.

Bring your images to life.

There are so many creative ways to bring a good photograph to life, sometimes the simplest of filters or "auto retouch" is all an image needs. However, there are thousands of Apps that will give you everything from cartoon effects to disco lights, from black and white to creative double exposures, scratched film to layering. When editing photos with filters, choose one or two, the old adage "less is more!"

Does quality matter?

The quality of the image is relative to the medium it will be displayed on. Larger images have larger file sizes and can slow down the loading times on your website or blog. For example, visitors with a slow internet connection might lose interest if the website takes too long to load! All of the major social media players like Facebook, Twitter, Instagram and Pintrest compress your images as soon as they are uploaded, to save space on their servers. Sites like 500pix and Flickr designate a space allowance and do not compress your images i.e. you get 1 GB of space for free and you choose the size of image to upload. If your primary objective is on-line marketing via Facebook, Instagram or Twitter, then an image shot and edited on your smartphone will be compressed via the platform during upload and will look excellent through out the platform when displayed. Flickr will allow you to upload the full image at maximum resolution which will be better for certain businesses and certain circumstances.

In general, the image quality shot by your camera,and compressed by Facebook is excellent and will get the job done, i.e. marketing your brand product or service.

Capturing

Before capturing always:

Make sure your phone is fully charged or at least has the charge you require to fulfil the task.

Make sure that you have enough memory to record and edit the required photographs. Depending on the settings, one photograph can require up to 25 MB.

Set your phone to flight mode so there are no incoming distractions.

Increase the screen's brightness up to maximum if capturing outdoors, if the light changes you want to be able to see your screen.

Be aware of where your phone's camera is located.

Ensure your hands do not cover the lens.

Most phones today come with two cameras, one at the front which is generally of a lower quality and a rear camera which is generally the main camera. The rear camera will have the larger sensor and in many cases, image stabilisation and a flash.

Simple Rules

1. Keep the camera as still as possible.
If you have a tripod, use it (you will need an adaptor!) If not, tuck your elbows tight into your side, hold the phone with both hands and in the moments before taking the shot hold

your breath to eliminate even the smallest of movements. In some cases, your breathing motion can effect the sharpness of your image - shots that require a slow shutter action like night/low light shots will be most effected.

2. Framing

The key concepts of framing or the basics of composing a shot. How you frame an image will greatly affect how balanced the shot feels. Below are the key rules of framing, take a trip to https://www.flickr.com/explore and look at the featured images, within them you will see these rules played out again and again.

2a. Portrait/Landscape framing

Both labels come from the classical art world, where portraits are painted with a narrow width and high height and landscapes are painted with a wide width and short height. Portrait is when your phone is standing tall, landscape is when your phone is held on its side. Both

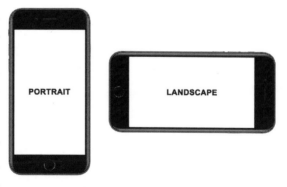

have advantages and context. In today's smart phone photo world, most shots are captured in portrait as this is the main way a phone is used and operated. Landscape, i.e. your phone titled 90 degrees, gives a nice shot for wide scenery shots. Traditionally, head-shots are portrait and landscapes/scenery shots are captured in landscape.

2b. Left to right

In the west, most languages write from left to right so when looking at a photograph, our eye naturally reads the image from left to right. Your image should always flow to the right, i.e. railway lines starting at the bottom left corner and moving to the top right, or a car moving from left to right. Reverse the rule for other languages, like Arabic.

2c. 80/20

Mainly applies to Landscape shots, the image should be made up of either 20% foreground and 80% background or 20% background and 80% foreground,i.e. the horizon should not be at the 50/50 across the centre of the image.

2d. Rule of thirds

Imagine your image as a grid, with two lines horizontal and two lines vertical. Where these lines meet,where they cross over are the points of interest, 4 in total . The rule of thirds is having two of these four points occupied by the main thing of interest.

2e. Leading Lines

Lines either real or implied which lead the viewers eye.

2f. Camera Positioning /Point of view

The most common image is taken from chest to eye height as it is easiest to see your screen from here when you're standing. Get creative; lie on the floor, crouch down low, angle your phone. Changing the angle can make a dramatic difference to your images.

2g. Symmetry and Pattern

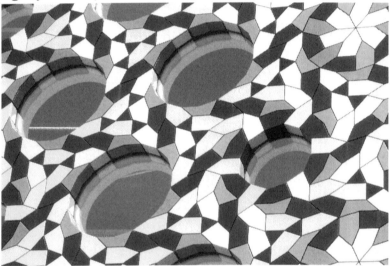

Not every image will have symmetry or pattern, however when capturing a scene that has a pattern, be sure to take advantage of it and include it in your composition, as patterns and symmetry are very pleasing to the eye and most often make a great image.

2h. Balance

Even when you follow the rules, your images may feel un-balanced, photography is an art and you should always go with what you feel, if it needs more give it more, if it needs less take something away.

2i. Cropping

Cutting an image back in the edit to eliminate any excessive distractions from your main points of interest. Sometimes this can't be done in camera at the time due to lens restrictions or physical obstacles.

3. Experiment

The only way to learn is to experiment. Luckily the phones digital memory allows you to take many photos and you can delete those that don't work.

Basics of camera control

Most of your shots will be taken using the smart phone cameras full auto mode. There are plenty of apps within both the Apple App store and Google's Play store that allow you to take control of the parameters/settings of your camera. As a rule, Android manufacturers bundle the phone with greater creative control and many ship with full manual controls within the native camera software. Apple's camera has limited manual controls built in but does have an exposure control live on screen when focusing, which can be quickly dragged up or down to increase or decrease the exposure of the shot.

1. Auto

Your smart phone camera features top of the line software that has been designed by very intelligent technicians and engineers. It will automatically gauge the light, the distance, the subject matter and decide on the best option available given the information presented. Setting your phone camera to 'Auto' is a safe bet and will deliver a well exposed picture 99% of the time. However, if you want more control and you are confident, there is always the freedom of manual controls. These can be accessed via your cameras native appor you can download an appropriate app to give you this control if required.

1a. Scene Mode

Scene modes are one step removed from 'full auto', they give you a theme to choose from and this theme determines the automation of the image being captured. Scene modes have names like night shot, sports mode, smile, through the glass and more. Each will set a specific combination of ISO, aperture, shutter speed and 'exposure' to get you the best results for your chosen scene. These modes, just like full auto are excellent and allow you to tell the camera what you are capturing. Although not native to some standard camera apps, there are plenty of options in the app stores.

2. Manual

Shooting in manual mode will give you full creative control over all the parameters of your smart phone camera. This is very exciting as most cameras, like DSLRs that give full manual controls are usually very expensive. Manual photography will allow you to take your photography to the next level and give you the creative options you need to fulfil your visions. A good way to start off in setting up manual shots is to allow the camera to take a picture in auto, then look at the picture and the auto settings the camera selected. **Photo Exif Editor** is a great app for seeing every last detail about an image.

Make a note of these and consider what you want to change, be it making the image brighter or sharper in certain areas or the overall colour tone or more depth to the focus. Using the auto settings generated by the camera, you can then move into manual mode and tweak the individual parameters to get the image results we desire. Remember to experiment, manual photography is always a dance between parameters. Below is a breakdown of each parameter, when using the manual controls you will be combining a combination of each of the settings to achieve your overall configuration.

2a. Exposure

Exposure is a combination of three manual controls - ISO, Aperture and Shutter speed. These three parameters control the amount of light that interacts with the sensor and therefore controls how bright your photo will be

2b. Shutter Speed

Shutter speed is how fast the shutter fires. The shutter lets light into the sensor so the faster the shutter operates at, the less light will get into the sensor. The longer the shutter speed,
the more light will get into the sensor due to the increased time the sensor is exposed to the light. A very fast shutter

speed will be used to freeze fast action, like a raft in a rapid or a boxer's punch. A very slow shutter speed will be used to create blurring motion or Milky water effects. For example, a fast shutter speed on a waterfall would catch all the spray and action of the water dead in its tracks, a slow shutter speed would give the appearance that the water was milky, silky and smooth.

2c. Aperture
Is a key component of how the camera controls light and therefore exposure. It is also the key to Depth of Field (Unfortunately DOF is simulated on phones with software.) DOF is the focus range, if the subject is in the range, it is in focus, if it lies outwith the range it will appear blurred.) Unfortunately, most apertures on smart phones are fixed, however this will change soon enough. The wider or larger the aperture (low number) the more light that comes in, this will allow better low light images i.e. shooting in poorly lit, indoors environments. It will allow a faster shutter speed and traditionally a shallower depth of field. A small aperture (high number) lets in less light, therefore the shutter speed will be slower to collect more light. This setting is good for landscapes,

getting everything in focus from in front of your camera all the way to the horizon. Apps like **Big Lens, Tadaa SLR phone** and **Snapseed** allow the user to create an artificial depth of field that aperture control would bring. The best phones have a fixed apertures as low as 1.7. The lower the better!

2d. ISO
Determines how sensitive the sensor is to light, ISO is the same as ASA from the analogue film era. Low ISO (low sensitivity) is always best. Use a higher ISO (high sensitivity) only when the light levels drop, because the higher the ISO, the more "grain" will be in your pictures.

2e. White Balance
Controls the colour temperature and affects how the camera reproduces the colours in the scene you are capturing. Playing with the manual white balance will give your scene more warmth or coolness. The apps with manual control will give either a selection of semi auto settings that are self explanatory i.e. sunny, cloudy, flash, indoors lamp, fluorescent lamp etc. Select the appropriate one for your current environment. The other option presented by manual apps is K values, the best advice for white balance is to use your eye to dial in the right settings or K value for your scene. K value is the colour temperature in Kelvin (Kelvin is a temperate measurement unit like Degrees Celsius).Compare what's in front of you and what is being displayed on the screen. When your happy lock

down (select) the K value.

2f. Basics of lighting
The flash is a powerful tool that can be used with great effect. Use the flash during the day to fill out a shot and makes shadows from the sun disappear. As a phone's flash is not impressively powerful, make sure the subject is in close range. For outdoor photography, use the sun as your light. Position your subject in relation to the sun to get the results you need (i.e. the sun behind you and in front/facing your subject, to light up their face.) Never take a shot directly into strong light, i.e. don't have your subject stand next to a window as they will disappear into darkness.

Things to note;

Models
If you have the budget to hire a model/models there are many agencies and a quick search in your location will reveal many options for your product. However, I always prefer using colleagues, friends, family members. First off it keeps your costs down and keeps the marketing unique, interesting and real.

Scenes
The setting of the scene will be outlined in your plan for the image. When planning, think about what you have at your disposal, i.e. business premises, your house, kitchen, garden, car etc and plan your scenes around these. There is no point in paying out cash to 'create' when you already have amazing scenes all around you.

Directing

You have planned your advert, you have booked a model or arranged a few colleagues to model your products, you have got some new product out of the wrapper, you have controlled the light and are ready to capture your images. Now you need to Direct the shot, you have the information of what you want to capture, of what you want to convey in the images, take time to communicate this to your models and remember you need to express your vision to them clearly so they can fulfil your idea. Communication is the key to directing a photo shoot.

Props

Again use props that are available and relevant.

Apps

There are thousands of camera apps available to replace or give you alternative to your current camera application. These are some of the best. However for the majority of shots, the native app is all you really need.

Iphone

Before trying any app that offers manual controls you must upgrade your software to IOS 8 or newer.(Check your version in settings)

- *VSCO Cam - Gives full manual control*
- *Manual - Gives full manual control*
- *Camera + - Gives full manual control*
- *Pro Camera 8 - Gives full manual control*

Android

Before trying any app that offers manual controls you must have upgraded your Android software to lollipop or newer.

67

(Check your version in settings.) Go to the Play store and install the 'Manual Camera Compatibility' app. This app will tell you which parameters your phone can manually control.

- *Manual Camera - Gives full manual control*
- *FV-5 - Gives full manual control even in older handsets!*
- *VSCO Cam - Gives full manual control*

Next level Solutions
A list of next level solutions can be found at www.smartphonemediaproduction.com

1. Smart phone Camera mount
There are many solutions available from simple grips to snap on cases, however the key components of the mounts are the same. The mount will allow you to mount your smartphone onto a tripod for stability.

2. Tripod
Allows for a steady shot, it allows you to take advantage of slower shutter speeds and the manual creativity that specialised camera apps can give. Especially good for sharp images, low light captures and landscapes.

3. Lenses
Lenses give you more options, and there are many options available for both Iphone and Android handsets. They come in the form of snap on lenses that can be applied to any phone and specialist cases with fully integrated lens mount systems. A lens will open up the scene in front of your phone, a wide angle lens will fit more into the image and a telephoto lens will bring objects from further afield closer to the sensor. Another option is a macro lens which gives you the ability to take ultra

close up shots.

4. Cases

There are more case options for the Apple phones as they have fewer handsets. However, you can find cases for almost all brands and models of Android phones to do whatever it is you want it to do. Case concepts include, tripod mountable protective cases (manfrotto), camera button cases, cases with interchangeable lens built in, cases with extra battery capacity and more.

5.Flash

External flash is one of the keys to professional photography as extra light allows you more control in any situation. There are options for small, external flashes that are triggered by your smartphone's own camera flash. These plug into your headphone socket.

6. Lights

Like a flash, lights give you more control of the environment and allow you to correctly expose for the scene you are capturing. There are many lighting options available. Small, portable, led lighting sets, that are reasonably priced and can light up a scene with ease. These can mount onto cases,tripods or just use a torch.

7. Sun Glasses

A simple hack, use your sun glasses to add an instant filter to your images if shooting outdoors in strong sun light. Shooting images should be fun, use everything at your disposal to get the shots you need.

8. Filters

Are used to change the colour of a scene or to bring out and define details. For example, Neutral Density Filters in a bright sky or sunset. Most filters for smartphones clip on for ease of use.

9. Selfie Stick

Not just a gimmick for taking excellent selfies, the stick can be used to get low shots (easy access), high shots (in crowds etc) and many angled shots that you wouldn't be able to access without it. These can be picked up extremely cheap and are sold in most supermarkets.

Editing

You are now ready to edit your photos. Within most of the apps already mentioned there will be the ability to edit and make minor adjustments to your images. Just be aware that a lot of the apps that are available offer in-app purchases but if you hunt around, you might find that level of feature in a different app for free. However, there are specialist apps for both Android and IOS that can give you all the manual creative editing that you want, as well as more general editing apps that can deliver you a huge variety of standardised filters and styles to give your images that extra jump with minimal work.

The main thing for the images that you capture is to get them up on to your social media sites and tag them with your website and any other relevant information, company address, booking info etc and get them working for you. However, if you want to take it to the next level you need to stamp them to make them identifiable with your brand/website/social media at a glance, so that when they are shared or viewed, it is very clear that they relate to your products and or services or at a minimum provide a traceable link that can bring curious customers to your online space. This is key, the smart phone gives you the power as a creative content producer but it also gives those that will copy and plagiarise your content that same power. In today's smart phone navigated web, there is a prevalence of users to screen grab images that they find interesting or appropriate for their own marketing use, to screen grab an image and then upload it to their own channel without any credit or link to your page, channel, website etc. This, unfortunately is on the rise. One way to make sure that your brand travels with your images is to stamp them. This is done in apps with a layering function.

The layering function allows you to place one photo on top of the other to combine parts of each photo into one image. Imagine real photos on your table, the bottom image is the image you have captured with the smart phone's camera, the image you layer on top of that is your brand identity. The brand image you layer on top of that should be mostly transparent. This transparent brand image should be saved in the .PNG file extension where most of the image can be transparent
:Samsung gallery app

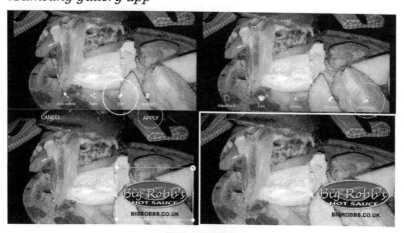

Apps
Layering Apps

Iphone
- *Juxtaposer or layrs*

Android
- *Samsung gallery app*
- *Photolayers*

Apps
There are hundreds from basic level all the way to industry standard to Photoshop! There are also hundreds of apps that will cartoonify, zombify your face (**Snapchat, Zombify**)to apps that can create instant art, from your images like **Lucid** and **Prisma.AI**, to graphic packages that make instant memes and posters like **Adobe Spark**. Don't be scared to use multiple apps to create your vision, i.e. converting a selfie using **Snapchat** into a strawberry face and then using an editing app to add a slogan or increase the redness of the image.

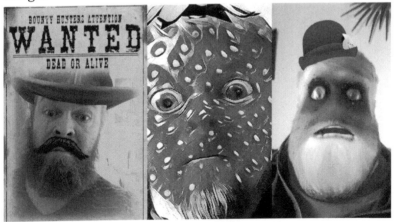

Standard Image Editing Apps
Iphone & Android

- *Snapseed*
- *Photoshop*
- *Pixlr*

The main editing features are available to play with in most photo editing apps.

Crop
Allows you to crop or trim the image, to lose unwanted features or just for better framing, symmetry etc.

Rotate
Allows you to rotate your image through 90,and 180 degrees. Some apps allow every any angle of rotation. Good if you have shot an image in landscape and you need to rotate it to portrait or fix the horizon line in a landscape image.

Brightness
Allows you to adjust the brightness of the shot.

Contrast
Allows you to adjust the difference between light and dark, a very important parameter.

Saturation
Allows you to adjust the intensity of the colour.

Sharpening
Allows you to sharpen the image, to make it more crisp.

Dodge
Allows you to lighten an area.

Burn
Allows you to darken an area.

Lens Blur
Allows you to artificially create an area of simulated lens blur.

Black and White
Allows you to de-saturate the entire image, removing all colour.

HDR
High Dynamic Range combines all the details from the shadows and highlights to give a very dramatic effect.

Vignette
Allows you to reduce the brightness of your images at their outer edge.

Frames
Allows you to add a graphical frame to highlight the image.

Distributing

The key to distribution of your images is using the platform or platforms that you are most in tune with. Assuming you are already using some form of social media, be it Facebook, Twitter, Instagram then upload your photos to them.

The key players in social media imaging are Facebook, Twitter, Instagram and Flickr. However, the key is to get your branded images on-line, if any of your customers are featured in the images tag them, tag your distributors, your sponsors, your partners and any other relevant person or company. Write a catchy tag line or header, write a short and precise body, that details what you are conveying in the image.

Eg Chef Tonies famous southern fried monk fish, every bite will have your mouth begging for more. Come on down and try it today, you wont be disappointed. For our full menu, opening times, prices and location, check our website @ . Keep up to date with our hot offers or excellent deals by simply liking our Fb page, following us on twitter and subscribing on Youtube #ChefTony #Food #Restaurant #Glasgow #BestinTown #1FREEbeerTUESDAYs. Please SHARE :)

This could be saved in a note app like **Google keep**, or held in the cloud using **Icloud, One drive, Google Drive**, then it can simply be copied and pasted to the end of each description.

Now when your images go on line to social media platforms like Facebook they will be good images, well thought out and relevant, they will be branded, have a catchy headline and description, indexed and search enabled (hash tags) with contact info, a prompt to buy, share and more. Compare that to an image that has been snapped and uploaded with no real thought behind it, it may go viral YES, but most probably it will disappear, or will never be associated with your product/service. This way, at least if it does go viral people know where to find you and your products/services.

Tracking

Using the options available on your chosen platform to record engagement between your images and your visitors. Use this information to make your images, tag lines, descriptions and any competitions etc more specific.

Video Cheat Sheet

 Battery Charged 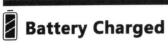**Flight Mode On**

Enough Memory **Screen Brightness**

Steady

Think Audio

Plan it

**Look @ lens
Selfies**

Light

Landscape

Size

Angle

Movement

Framing

Choose your shots - Size, Angle, Movement, Frame

Video

If a photograph can convey a thousand words with one image, then a video can potentially convey a million words with a short video presentation. Film, as a medium has been in use for over 100 years and in that time it has been used to convey every kind of emotion, behaviour, action, product etc.

Video is a beautiful marriage of moving images and audio, most of the information from the previous chapters are extremely relevant when working with video. Audio, image rules and next level solutions cross over to video.

Video, in one format or another is the future!! It is the future of the internet and the future of internet marketing. Video is the last of the mainstream media platforms to break the grips of the ruling corporate class. It is now available to all, to empower the common man, be it used for the dissemination of information for activists, educators or entrepreneurs, the fact is that the production and distribution of video is now available and open to all.

Like audio and photography, video has entire social media communities built around it. Your videos, once captured, are easy to share and easy to brand. It is also a very exciting time to be creating video. Right now (2016), every major social media platform is investing in and prioritising video, the big players like **YouTube** and **Vimeo** are now seeing fierce competition from the non traditional video platforms, like **Facebook, Instagram, Vine, Snapchat** and **Twitter**. These social media giants are trying to capitalise on the fantastic advertising revenue, the high engagement and the upward trend of increasing video consumption by prioritising video on their networks. In this section we will cover the basic rules and ideas of video creation, planning the video, capturing the shots, editing it together, as well as adding your logos/brands, adding filters, tagging and distribution.

Please don't be put off by how deep the potential is for video. You don't have to start with a masterpiece, start small and simple and as your experience grows in video capture and editing, progressively make your videos more complicated.

Worked Example
A restaurant owner - Video orientated example.

Below I will outlay some of my ideas on how I would utilise and leverage the smartphone to build a buzz around a restaurant. This is only one example of almost limitless possibilities for the pocket powerhouse.

Plan, Capture, Edit, distribute and Track.

Plan
Each new video will be captured, edited with intro and outro graphics, uploaded, tagged, # hash tagged with description. Each video between 15 and 30 seconds. Each video is an opportunity to infuse the video with passion! Passion for food, ingredients, kitchen techniques etc, passion that will fill the restaurant up with food lovers looking to experience this passion translated into excellent food.

Video ideas
1.   Use video to highlight the quality products and services

provided by the restaurant.
2. A full video menu for the restaurant.
3. Kitchen tips and Kitchen basics
4. Exploring local markets with the chef.

Capture

1. Use video to highlight the quality products and services provided by the restaurant. Simple videos that open up the expertise behind the scenes to customers, highlight the high quality foods and services available. Highlighting the freshest ingredients, butchery, fish mongers, busy nights, busy Kitchen, customer service and customer reviews.

2. The video menu would be sharp montage of the ingredients, kitchen prep and the final dish. This would all be in a video that lasts less than 20 seconds. Gives the customer a glimpse of the passion, time and expertise that goes into preparing their FRESH meals.

3. Recipes, kitchen tips, kitchen basics video series. Short sharp bits of industry knowledge to make the life of our customers better and at the same time establishing us as industry leaders and experts in our field. This video series will show off and celebrate our food, our kitchen's technical ability, our facilities and our all round expertise. 30 seconds max.

4. Out and about, exploring local markets, buying fresh ingredients - give the customer the idea that we go out of our way to source the best, that we live the food we create, that this is more than a meal, that this is our lifestyle. That's the kind of place I want to eat. 5 minute max.
Remembering the importance of audio in the video experience, I would make capturing good audio environments a priority,

as well as supplementary audio of key sounds. For example, a pan sizzling, knifes chopping, the lively buzz of the restaurant, laughter etc.

Create a process to allow videos to be made to a standardised formula.

Example

'Video Menu'

1. Intro with restaurant brand and web address -This could be an image. (3 seconds),
2. Ingredients - images or video (5 seconds)
3. Prep - images or video (5 seconds)
4. Final dish - images or video (5 seconds)
5. Brand and web address - Image (3 seconds)
6. Please share - Title or image or video (3 seconds)

All footage to be shot close up or medium close up, edited in **Premier Clip** (or your Favourite editing app)and then uploaded to the company's Facebook page with the appropriate title, description and tag.

This simple standard for the 'Video Menu' could then be learned by any member of the team, ensuring a uniformed style and production standardised for all of the restaurant's videos. Create a simple word document (**Google docs)** or give a simple presentation on how this should be implemented, making sure that all staff are happy with independently replicating the formula, using their own or the company's phone.

Edit

All captured footage should be edited directly on the phone, using your preferred app. Every video should show the restaurant's brand and contact details, before being distributed on-line.

Distribute
I would select a few key social media platforms that are best placed for video. To start with, I would be uploading to YouTube and Facebook. Video eat lots of mobile data allowance so make sure you're on WIFI if you have a limited data plan. As with photography and audio, I would copy and paste my pre-prepared business description and sales copy into the end of each uploaded video's description.

Track
Keeptrack of the videos via YouTube and Facebook's analytics to see how engaging the videos are, what works and what could be better.

After road testing a few sample items for his new video menu, the restaurant manager found it to be an instant success and he sees a dramatic spike in engagement on his social media pages with many shares and new subscribers. The customers love the short, sharp videos showing the sensational food they could be enjoying this evening if they just booked a table! They tag them and share them and as a result, bookings increase. Two of the restaurants signature chicken dishes go viral, engaging and gaining comments from across the globe. The manager/owner realises the value of the video menu and commits to setting aside a small amount of time each day to catalogue all of the food and beverages served within the establishment. Working within the original plan and the framework that has proven successful, the manager is planning his next project already.

Ok, lets get into it.

<u>Treatment</u>

Outline your entire treatment for the planned project and update it as your plan comes together.

<u>Planning</u>

As the nature of video is potentially unlimited, one must have a plan for it's use.

The simplest plan in video is called a "story board". This is a simple, visual, shot by shot progression that shows what you are aiming to capture. Think, comic book!! Don't worry if you can only draw stick men, it's about getting the ideas out and building a framework for creating awesome videos, not a drawing competition.

There are plenty of drawing apps like Audtodesk Sketchbook for drawing out your story boards or you can just use a pen and paper.

Things to consider

Switch camera to Flight Mode

Don't get distracted whilst you are being creative. The world isn't going anywhere.

What is video?

When we create video we must consider the audience, they are the ones who will be watching the story. The visuals that you chose, the order you put them in, the audio you use etc will all come together to make the video. Your audience is essentially a passive participant. You have the vision, you need to choose the best way to represent your vision, to gain maximum engagement.

What is being made?

Think about the end result, what is it that you want the video to achieve? Is it a sales video? Is it an information product? Is it just eye candy to keep customers informed, a short film to promote Halloween, a photo montage, a talking head, an interview etc etc. Is it advertising a service, a product, an upcoming event or social proofing in the form of customer testimonials, mentors, celebrity endorsements etc. The list of possibilities is endless. I recommend that you **ALWAYS** have a plan for video!!

The most common smartphone video!

Is a continuous, single take, filmed in portrait, that is uploaded with no editing. This is good and if the content is good, you are half way there. However, most professional videos are shot in landscape and are a collection of shorter videos (think cinema or TV). So keep the enthusiasm and the great content, lets just make the production that little bit better. This could be as simple as adding your brand to the beginning and a call to action at the end.

A collection of videos

Video is like a photographer's slide show, in that it is a collection of shorter videos that is stitched together to convey a story. Load up a video and watch for the cuts, the changes between two pieces of footage. A good edit will never be seen (unless you intentionally look for it) and a bad edit will be obvious (more on this later.) Think about the different ways you can creatively show the product. Change angles, look for flow etc. Think about this when your planning.

Plan it out it or go freestyle?
Only go freestyle once you have successfully planned and completed a video project, one that you have now transformed into a template. Within this framework, you can begin to freestyle. Or put another way, once you have a firm grasp of the basics try going freestyle. But learn the basics first.

Bring your video to life.
Just like photography, there are so many creative ways to bring your videos to life. However, unlike photography the over use of filters in video can instantly seem gimmicky, amateurish and cheap, mainly because the high end VFX (visual effects- e.g. spaceships, lasers, sky replacement, computer generated animals etc) we are used to in movies are clearly very different from anything your phone can provide. Most of the time, no filters are needed. However, there are thousands of apps that will give you everything from cartoon effects to disco lights, from black and white to zombie face warps. There is a time and a place for filters and if it's in your plan, then utilise them to get the look and feel you have envisioned. But remember,over use or the wrong use can make your video look cheap and tacky. It is a continuous learning experience but you are in control. The main filter I use is a simple colour filter to bring some warmth or some coolness to a scene. Like music, colour can change the feel of a video.

Does quality matter?
The quality of the video is relative to the medium it will be viewed through. More and more content is being consumed on the phone and almost all smartphones come with a high resolution screen. To take advantage of this and give the viewer the best experience possible, I recommend full HD (1080) or standard HD (720). Higher resolutions, mean larger file sizes,

and large files can slow download times on your website or blog.

All of the major social media players like **YouTube, Vimeo, Facebook, Twitter** and **Instagram** will give you multiple compression options for your video. Most standard smartphones will now automatically record in Full 1080HD (which is 1920 by 1080 pixels), or 720 HD (which is 1280 by 720 pixels). Some phones even film in Ultra HD or 4K. As 4k is still in its infancy and with very few people being able to access it (owning a 4k screen), I would recommend staying away from it for now. The higher the resolution, the more data (data allowance) you will require to get it uploaded and then for your customer to download it. If uploading in HD, be sure to use your WIFI connection as video will eat you mobile data quickly.

Branding your videos

I would plan to add a short intro graphic with the business brand and contact details, no more than 2 or 4 seconds at the beginning of every video. This is important for many reasons;

1. Instantly makes your customers associate with your brand etc.

2. It looks more professional.

3. In todays auto play, especially on Facebook where videos play automatically, even if a customer doesn't watch your video, as they scroll down their time line they may see (due to autoplay)your intro graphic and brand, this my be enough to entice them into watching the rest of the video. This intro can be a short video of your brand, it could be your logo animated, a simple image with brand and web address or a highlight of the videos contents.

Short attention span

Cut the dead wood, no one wants to watch you babble about something that is non related to the product, service or event your advertising in the title. No one wants to watch a video that starts and finishes with you fumbling to press record or saying "oh I think its recording". Your video should be short, snappy, and as succinct as possible. Having a good plan helps keep you on track and stop the waffle.

Video length

As we are completing the whole process on the smartphone I would aim to keep each video between 15 and 60 seconds long, this is simply due to the memory that video uses. We are now seeing the addition of plus 100GB handsets but at the moment (2016) the average is between 16 and 32GB which is enough. 1080 full HD will use around 200mb per minute.720 HD will use around 80mb per minute. Always make sure you have enough space for your capture and remember, the phone also needs space to edit (i.e. duplicate and move video around.)

Before capturing, make sure you have the space needed. If your phone is full, take a moment to back it up (if required) and then delete any old videos, photos and audio to free up space for your latest project. I would recommend a minimum of around 5 GB of free space. You can back up (using Wifi) to various free cloud storage facilities like, Googles drive, Microsoft's One drive and I-cloud.

The Power of Music

Music changes a scene dramatically. When choosing your music, ask yourself how does your chosen music make you feel? Does it match the intended mood or intended feel of the video?. Imagine a simple video of a man walking up to the gate of a house. A women inside looks out of the window to see the man. By playing the classic music from Jaws, we would instantly think the man was sinister and was at the gate to do harm in some way. If we changed the music to something upbeat and inspirational we may assume he was her lover or a friend or non threatening stranger. Music has the power to change the entire feel of a video, choose yours wisely.

What is at stake?

Emotion is one of the keys to good content! For your video, photo etc to sell a service, bring a new product to the market or highlight a social injustice, then you must bring the emotion. Laugh, smile, shout, express! Ask yourself 'What is at stake?'. Videos with no emotion will not resonate as well with their audience, as videos with emotion.

Mobile content consumption is increasing!

As noted in the introduction, the consumption of video is moving swiftly from desktops and laptops to mobile. Making video specifically for mobile consumers is therefore the key. At the moment, the only major factor this changes is the importance of your intro for social media networks' auto play functions. For example, Facebook automatically plays videos on your timeline as you scroll down your news feed, make the first 10 seconds of your videos captivating, and they may stop scrolling and watch.

Capturing

Most phones come with two cameras, both cameras should be capable of shooting 720 HD and more likely full 1080 HD. The rear camera on high end phones will additionally come with a better lens, optical image stabilisation or at least digital image stabilisation and an LED light. Stabilisation is a crucial part of video capture. Optical Image Stabilisation - is mechanical and is done using the phone's optics. Digital Image Stabilisation - is done digitally by the phone's software.

Simple Rules
A lot of the rules for capturing images (refer to the last chapter) also apply to video, so consider them as well as the list below.

1. Kill background apps
Kill all background apps to make sure your video recording is getting your phone's full attention (processing power and RAM).

2. Keep the camera as still as possible
If you have a tripod, use it (you will need an adaptor to connect your phone, these are extremely cheap) If not, tuck your elbows tight into your side, use both hands and in the moments before taking the shot hold your breath, you move when you breath or use something steady to hold your phone against, like a table or tree.

Stabilisation really is a top priority when shooting video, some high end phones now come with built in optical image stabilisation, which takes the jarring and shakiness out of your video. However, to make your video as professional as possible always be aware of stabilisation and your motion when capturing video.

3. Audio is the most important!
Most people unfortunately assume that the image is the most important aspect of a video. However, AUDIO is king, be it your voice, background noise, music etc. You must be completely attentive to the audio you are capturing.

4. Follow your plan/storyboard

Take the time to draw out your ideas Stick men are fine. Most videos are a collection of shorter videos.

5. Framing

All rules with regards to framing, balance, symmetry etc are incorporated into your decision when you begin to make a video. However, added to this we have to think about the balance and progression of each shot to the next in the sequence. 'Cutting' shots together in editing is fairly simple and a lot easier when following a planned storyboard.

6. Shot sizes, Camera angel, Camera movement

When framing your video capture, you have four key components to consider; the shot size, the camera angle, the movement of the camera and the framing/composition, which was described in the photography section. Watch your favourite TV dramas or movies and observe the shot sizes, angles, movement and framing used by the director to convey their message to the audience. The more you watch and practice, the more experience you will gain.

7. Shot Sizes

There are many different shot sizes used to convey different qualities and elicit different reactions from the audience. The progression from one shot to another is called a cut.

7a. Extreme close up

This is a good shot for showing detail, like the emotions in someone's eyes or a tear running down a face. It is also used to highlight fine details in a scene. The

ECU hides the wider picture and focuses on details we would normally not see, it magnifies and is used for dramatic effect.

7b. Close up

This is a another good shot for showing detail but it is not as extreme as the ECU, its more natural and is used to show details, as well as convey trust, allowing you into the person or item's personal space.

7c. Medium close up

This is usually shot from the top of the chest and upwards, revealing a little more. It is close but not too close and is a good shot size for parts of interviews, emotional reactions, facial expressions, all whilst giving the viewer a little bit more of the surroundings.

7d. Medium shot

This is usually shot from the waist up, to just above the head but can also be from the knees to above the head. This and the wide shot are the most common shot for a beginner as it's a natural shot

that does not intrude into personal space like the ECU, CU. The shot can used as a single shot with one person framed or as a two or three shot, each framing more people. It is also the most common shot size used for over the shoulder shots. This shot size is good for interviews, it's the general shot size you would use when you have used your wide to establish the scene and used your close ups to hide the scene or focus on detail. Once the surroundings and finer details have been established, we revert back to the medium shot.

7e. Wide shot

A great shot that begins to show subject, in relation to the surroundings, showing the true size of the person in relation to their surroundings and establishes more of the surroundings. The shot covers the whole body from below the feet to above the head.

7f. Long shot

In Westerns, it is used as the opening scene, it establishes the space, the surroundings, showing the subject in relation to the surroundings. It shows action rather than emotion and is used as an establishing shot or to set the scene. Good for landscapes, exterior shots, scenery, capturing the crowd or a conference/on stage presentation.

7g. Extra long shot
This is the same as the long shot but more dramatic in nature.

8. Camera angle
The camera angle can dramatically change what is being captured.

8a. Birds eye view
As the name suggests, the shot is from directly above the scene, giving a dramatic change in perspective and can be used to show how things in the scene are connected. Combined with

movement to create God shots i.e. from a God-like position and is used a lot with a long shot to convey action. This is a very popular angle used in popular/viral cooking videos.

8b. Point of View
This angle is filmed from where the character's eyes would roughly be and is used to convey the scene from the character's perspective.

8c. Over the shoulder A & B
This angel is mainly used with a medium shot size, however it can be used with any shot size and is used to

convey interaction between characters. The different shot sizes combined with this angle gives you plenty of variety to convey emotion as well as actions from this angle.

8d. High angles

This is a great establishing shot. It is not as extreme as the bird's eye view and is used to make things/ characters look weak, submissive, or frightened. When used as a point of view, it looks down on the  subject, giving power to the POV character. This angle is combined with a variety of shot sizes to convey the power relationship between characters.

8e. Low angles

This is used to show dominance or strength of the character on screen and from a POV, it can be used to convey the weakness of the character's perceptive. It can be used to make the POV  actor look weak, submissive, frightened, or to indicate that they are in a predicament.

8f. Angled or Dutch

Off horizon, odd angled shots are used a lot in horror and action scenes as they are good for bringing drama and confusion, as well as being able to mask the surroundings and conceal information in a scene.

9. Camera movements

Camera movement brings a lot to the screen. In Hollywood level productions, shots are rarely captured without movement. Below are the basics.

9a. Pan

It moves across the horizontal axis. For smooth pans you will need a tripod or a gimbal.

9b. Tilt

It moves across the vertical axis, i.e. from the floor to ceiling, or in reverse from the character's head to their toes. For a smooth tilt you will need a tripod or a gimbal.

9c. Push in

The camera pushes in towards the scene, for example if the shot starts wide, it could push into a medium shot. This is used in interviews to convey that the interviewee is telling the truth, also used in product shots.

9d. Pull out

The opposite of a push in, the camera movement pulls out away from the subject and is used to covey that an interviewee is lying or is not to be trusted. It is also used in product shots.

9e. Crane or dolly

These are pieces of equipment used to give big, smooth sweeping movements to a shot. Due to the high cost of this equipment, they are used mostly in big budget productions.

9f. Drones

Drones can be used to create grand crane like movements from angles like birds eye and and high angle.

9g. Gimbals

These can be used to create smooth pan and tilt movements, as well as smooth walking or gliding shots.

10. Shot list

Make a list of the key shots you want when filming, be it a product advert, an event or a protest. Opening Shot, Establishing Shots, Creative Shots, Action shot and a Closing shot. Always tell a story and show a progression, never have the same two shots back to back.

11. Shot Order

Not everything is shot in sequence, if you have five shots to make your product video, in two different locations (ie the kitchen and the restaurant floor, three shots in one and two shots in the other). Plan to shoot those shots from each location back to back even if they are out of order from your storyboard. Video is often shot out of order and put back together in the desired order in the edit. This is where a well thought out plan/storyboard becomes key.

12. Light it up

Good lighting is key to both photography and video. If it's dark, switch a light on. Most video apps allow the phones LED flash to be used as a video light, if it is dark use it.

13. Takes

Very rarely do you get the shots you want the first time you film a scene, always be willing to shoot the take again.

14. Front facing camera

If you are shooting a selfie styled video blog - don't look at the screen - look at the LENS, so your eyes meet the audience on screen and you don't appear to be looking down.

15. Never Zoom
Zooming is a feature that is rarely seen in professional work and when it is, it always has a purpose. However, it is almost always seen in amateur and low cost productions. Don't zoom, step closer or step away for the shot you need.

16. Ground markers
Use coloured tape or chalk marks on the ground (make sure it is out of shot), to ensure actors are positioned where they need to be. This ensures they are framed how you need them to be.

17. Experiment
It is the only way to learn - practice, practice, practice.

Basics of camera control

1. Auto modes
Most of your videos will be created using full auto mode. It is the easiest, most effective way to "shoot and go" with video. Just like photography, there are a number of apps available that will give you extra control.

2. Auto
The auto mode in the native apps are excellent, written and programmed by very intelligent technicians and engineers. It will automatically gauge the light, the subject and decide on the best option available given the information presented. In most cases with today's smart phone video cameras, the software 'Auto' is a safe bet and will deliver a well exposed video, time and time again.. However, if you want more control and you are comfortable and confident, you can take it

to the next level with manual controls.

3. Manual modes
The various manual functions are described in the photography section. The major differences for video, is that these settings are now being applied over time.

Things to note

Directing
Again, deals with bringing everything together, it is the art of holding the reins and directing everyone who is involved (or just yourself) to get your vision completed. This takes clear communication, planning, a shot list and patience.

Actors
A good actor can bring a lot of value to your brand, they can also bring the motion, emotion, , passion, humour, confidence etc that your vision requires. If you have no budget for an actor use a family member or colleague to convey your message the best they can. You never know they me be the next Arnie!!

Scenes
For a photo shoot, you may have to create just one scene, for a short promo you may make up two or three different scenes, depending on your creative vision for the project. Keep things simple, keep everyone who is involved in the project in the loop. With good communication, everything will run smooth.

Props
Use props that are available and relevant. Use your products and use your own equipment. Most of the time you won't have to actually buy props, the trick is to improvise, this is the true

art of film making.

Apps for capturing
There are thousands of apps, you can get lost in the app stores. These are some of the best, **however for most the native app is all you will ever need.**

Iphone
Before trying any app that offer manual controls you must upgrade your software to IOS 8 or newer.

- *Filmic Pro*
- *Kinomatic Video Camera: Pro Cam*
- *Camcorder x - profesional video*
- *Filmakr - manual video camera*

Android Camera
Before trying any app you must have upgraded your software to Lollipop or newer. Then go to the play store and install the 'Manual Camera Compatibility' app. This app will tell you which parameters your phone can manually control.

- *Filmic Pro*
- *Manual Camera*
- *FV-5*
- *VSCO Cam*

Something different
The thing about mobile film making is it's pace. New, game changing Apps appear daily. An example is **Snapchats lenses,** which give you the sort of power that was only found in a Holywood VFX department 5 years ago. Snapchats facial mapping engine is incredible and it allows you to map almost

anything to your face, capture it in video mode all in real time. I have used it to create short humorous videos. **Snapchat video** allows for a maximum of 10 seconds recording for each video, however you can edit multiple videos together, to create your video. Always be on the look out for new trends, new ideas, new apps, mobile video is a creative place that is changing up the rules.

Next Level solutions
A list of next level solutions can be found at www. smartphonemediaproduction.com

Recap from Audio and Photography
External microphone, Camera mount case, Tripod, Lenses, LED Light, Filters.

1. Batteries
If you are shooting continuous video for a blog, social media post or multiple scenes for a product promo, you are going to need ample battery. Most android handsets allow the user to purchase extra batteries, however Apple do not. The easiest and best solution is an external portable power supply, which can be plugged into your phone to give it that crucial charge. These are usually called "Power Banks".

2. Professional Choices.
Your smartphone can be fixed to most traditional options using a 'smartphone to tripod mount'.

2a. Gimbal
These are also known as electronic steady cams. These give you super smooth footage even when running, walking, etc.

A small computer and motors stabilise your movement along 3 axis (X,Y and Z) to create super smooth Hollywood like movement. Smartphone gimbals are small and handheld. They are expensive but provide instant professional polish to your shots. I take mine everywhere!!

2b. Steady cam
Same idea as an electronic Gimbal but mechanical, these are generally cheaper and fiddly. These work on the principles of counter balance and again give your video a smooth, steady, professional feel, even when walking. Small and easy to transport.

2c. Slider
A professional slider allows you to get a nice controlled shot as the camera moves across a fixed plane (usually the horizontal x axis). Sliders typically come in lengths between 60 and 120cm, once you have fixed your smartphone to the sliding plate, you can smoothly move the phone along the fixed plane of the slider for that ultra smooth shot. These come in manual and motorised versions.

2d. Jib or swing arm
The swing arm gives you the ability to create large sweeping shots, that instantly takes your video from looking 'low budget' to high gloss professional. It looks like a miniature construction crane, which is mounted on a tripod. At one end you mount your smartphone and at the other a counter weight. Swing arms are typically between 2 and 4 metres in length.

2e. Drone
A small remote controlled helicopter that can give you the ability to fly through, fly over, fly around and more, for that

big budget cinematic feel. Can be expensive but the price is continuously falling.

2f. Boom pole

Allow the sound operator to swing the mic out just above the frame of the video to capture the best audio possible. It is essentially a long pole that allows a microphone to be attached, you will need a long mic cable for this. The boom pole can also be used with a gimbal to get some truly spectacular shots.

The professional equipment listed above will take a good few dry runs to master their movements etc. Experiment, experiment, experiment.

All the best gear and great tech in the world will not automatically make your video better. The key is, as always a well structured story, great content and great value for your customer. Once you have a great concept/ story etc then you can think about making your production super slick with these high end solutions but do not substitute great content for poorly shot drone footage, because you will just be wasting own and your customers time. As a lecturer once said to me ,

"Robb it doesn't matter that the college doesn't have x,y,z equipment because your story is rubbish and until you fix it, no equipment or fancy tech will be able to help you or it!"

Editing

Your customers are not looking for perfection they are looking for your products and services. If your content is good (and after following my ideas, it should be), then your customers, your audience will forgive any faults for good quality content about your products and services. So don't delay. Content is king. But just to clarify, content and great production is best.

Like every new skill, editing will get better with practice. When you are editing in your app of choice, you will not lose the original clips that you captured, the apps will work with a copy and your original footage will always be accessible. So don't be scared to practice. (This is why you need to have space clear on your phone).

Video editing is probably the most intensive process your phone will ever do!! If you are not using a premium high end Smartphone, you may find the software stuttering, this is to be expected. Give it a few seconds to recover or reduce the amount of effects etc you have layered. Always make sure you kill all background apps before launching your video editing app, this way your app of choice will be able to take full advantage of your phones CPU and RAM.

So what is video editing?

Video editing is the process of joining together multiple video clips (these can be created from a single video or from multiple videos) to tell your story visually. The 'cut' is where two videos are stitched together. In a well edited video you don't see the edit, it is seamless, you just experience the story. It is the mechanism through which the story is conveyed. However, bad editing can take the viewers out of the video and make them focus on the cuts.

Homework

It is a simple task, just be a conscious observer in everything you watch on TV, online etc. Watch for the cuts, the different shots used between each cut, count them etc. You might be surprised to realise how many cuts can make up a short scene!

Terminology of the edit.

1. Import
Is to bring the footage that you intend to use into the app.

2. Export (share, HD, Quality)
Once you have finished your edit, you will export it to a single video. The App will compile the audio, video, titles, filters, effects etc and output a video ready for you to share on-line. The export settings will allow you to chose the output quality, usually between 720 HD and 1080 HD. Most free apps will stamp the final video with their own watermark (usually small) which can be removed with their paid version.

3. Footage
The videos you have captured for the project can be reviewed and renamed in the phone's native video gallery or file explorer app before editing. Renaming files from 0001.mp4 to ModelAtDoor.MP4, 0002.mp4 to CloseUpProduct.MP4 and so on. This helps keeps your project organised, especially handy for larger projects.

4. Audio
A voice over, a music track, sound effects all need to be imported. I recommend keeping your audio in .MP3 as it is the most common file format and all video apps will be able to use them.

5. Text/Titles
Titles are created in the editing app, used for introducing the brand, subject, telling the story etc. Most editing apps have a selection of pre-made titles that come with animated transitions to give a professional feel. Titles are made up of the

word being displayed, its font, its size, its colour, its location on screen and its animation in and out.

6. B Role
This refers to the "other footage" you shot on the day, i.e. the B Role. For example, the main footage could be of an interview with a chief, the B Footage would be lots of shots of the chief cooking, cleaning, getting emotional, his creations etc . This B Role footage would be cut into the interview to give it context, to give it emotion, to bring the interview to life.

7. Time line
Is the key place in every editing app, where you create, trim, combine and layer your audio, video and titles. It displays the progress of your video footage over time.

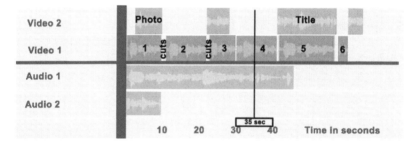

8. Sequence of shots
This is placing or introducing your footage to your time line in the order that the shots will be played. In most apps, the clips can simply be dragged into your preferred order, before you trim them.

9. Cuts
Comes from the original film days, when film needed to be cut physically. It refers to where your footage is cut. For example

a 3 minute video may have a shaky start up to the 30 second mark, from 30 seconds onwards the footage is perfect. The cut would be just after the 30 second mark, after the unwanted content. You would then select the unwanted section and delete it.

10. Trim
Just like trimming a hedge, very similar to the cut function, the difference is you would drag it from say
0 seconds to 32 seconds, when the footage becomes usable. The trim gives further adjustment to your cut and is the main tool used to adjust footage in mobile editing apps. Some editing apps allow you to select a time and trim everything to the right or left of this selection, which is a really useful feature.

11. Effects
From black and white to film grain, these are applied at the end of the editing process just before
exporting. Effects and filters are great fun to play with but remember that most often than not 'less is more'.

12. Transitions
Blends two shots together with style, from subtle fades to fancy swipes, as well as transition shapes and 3D transitions. Less is more when it comes to editing, remember editing should be invisible. A good editing app will allow you to select the amount of time a transition lasts for, a nice cross fade(a simple transition fading two clips together) should be between 0.5 seconds and 2 seconds long (i.e. the time it takes to complete the transition between the two shots) depending on the effect you are attempting to achieve.

13. Colour Control

The ability to tint a video with a particular colour or increase the brightness or contrast levels is extremely powerful. Using a colour filter can instantly change the mood and feel of a video and using brightness adjustments can instantly bring dull footage back to life. Colour and adjustments should be done near the end of your edit after everything else is in place.

14. Time

Video footage can be slowed down and sped up to create dramatic effect. For example, a static shot of a road side junction at night or a cloud filled sky filmed at normal speed when sped up will look dramatic. Slowing the video down over time can create equally dramatic effects, a popular shot is of a dog running or close ups of people eating.

15. Themes

Some apps have automated themes that layer titles, effects, colour adjustments and music to your footage to get great, interesting results fast. These can then be pushed into full manual mode for further tweaking.

15. Auto Edit

Some apps even auto edit your selected footage. These can be fun for action shots or family videos where the audio (voice capture, background sounds etc) is irrelevant, as everything on the time line will be mixed to a sound track. In this instance, you select the footage and a song (from their selection or from your phone) and the app does the rest. It can be a hit or miss but they will only get better. The best thing by far about auto edit is they always produce a finished video!! **Fastcuts** and **Quik** are two excellent apps.

Top Tip
1. No storyboard

If you don't have a story board, and your thinking fast on your feet, follow each new shot by a different shot!! Change the size, location, angle, etc of each new shot. This will keep your video visually interesting.

2. The editor has power

The video editor has the ultimate control over how a video will look and feel. Their choice of music, their choice of titling, the length of shots used, the order of the shots, the transitions, the colour etc can drastically alter the original vision. The editing process is the ultimate in creative control, and it is where a video is **made great or made bad.**

3. What is the video about?

There is one key question that you should always have in mind as you begin to edit your video together. What is the video about? Or what is it's purpose? From this question you will be better informed to select the appropriate music, pacing, titling etc to fit your answer. Fast heavy metal music combined with jagged title fonts, edited to a furious pace is never going to be the best idea for a short coffee shop advert to emphasise it's relaxed atmosphere and excellent customer service. Everything within your video should come together and compliment each other to produce the finished video.

4. Emotion and emotional arks

Stories always highlight emotion, be it sadness or happiness, anger or fear - use emotional footage that you have captured, inter cut with B roll footage to lengthen the emotional impact of those clips.

5. Pacing
Select the appropriate style of music for the video you are making.

6. Edit to the beat
A popular shortcut to editing is to select either the beat or key instrumental changes to edit to. This has the effect of synchronising the footage and the music and is almost always complimentary. This is in essence what the auto edit apps do.

7. Problem Solving
Welcome to the world of editing. Editing is where you solve the problems that you never planned for. There is almost always a creative way to increase the emotional impact of a scene or bring branding to a video or remove a background item. When using a desktop editing package like Premier Pro, anything is possible but until the mobile apps catch up, a little creative thinking will be needed. I regularly use two or three different editing apps to get the features I need for a project. For example **Quik** has excellent titles so I create them here, **Filmorago** has some excellent filters and overlays so I may finish the video in this app. The key is to think outside the box, on my website I have many examples of videos that I have shot and edited as well as links to other fantastic videos shot and edited on the humble smartphone.

Apps
As a professional video editor I use **Adobes Premier Pro**, the Adobe Premier mobile editing app is FREE, it is super simple to navigate, fast and comes with the basic creative options and for me seamlessly integrates with the desktop application. However, most of the time I use **KineMaster** to make the film as it is as close to a full editor as is currently

available.

IOS
- *Adobe Premier Clip - Basic and powerful*
- *I Movie - Basic and powerful*
- *FilmoraGo - Themes, Text options and more*
- *Quick - By Gopro - Great for simple automated videos to music.*

Android
- *Adobe Premier Clip - Basic and powerful*
- *FilmoraGo - Themes, Text options and more - A little fiddly but has lots of creative options*
- *KineMaster - This is the most complete video editor for Android.*
- *Quick - By Gopro - Great for simple automated videos to music.*

Distributing

Most editing apps have a function to directly upload to YouTube, Facebook and other social media channels. I always save and export my videos to my phone's memory first, as this allows me to view the finished article to decide if it needs some more adjustments, before giving it the green light to be uploaded.

For video, my main channels are YouTube and Facebook as they have the best tools for distribution and the best communities built around video.

Tracking

Again, use the various statistics generated by your chosen platform to see how your community is engaging with your videos. With video, one of the key metrics used by both

YouTube and Facebook to gauge popularity is not video likes or views but video play time or engagement.

Example : 1)A short two minute video with 300 views with each viewer engaging for the full two minutes 2) A six minute long video with 4000 views with each viewer engaging for an average of thirty seconds of the six minutes.

Example one is what you're looking for, ie full engagement with your video content. Engagement ranks better on sites like YouTube. However, example two has something that is brining in the viewers, it is not keeping them hooked but it is bringing them in. Combine what is working from both videos, i.e. a great 'hook' and great content to keep your viewers engaged in your new video.

Always use the information generated from your videos to inform your viewers of your next video creation.

Live Video Cheat Sheet

 Battery Charged   **Lens not the screen**

 Wifi/Data   **Screen Brightness**

Advertise it

Plan it

Think Audio

Portraite

Camera Person

Steady

Count it in

Profesional

Branding

111

Live Video

This is a fairly new feature that allows you to stream live video from your phone, host a seminar, broadcast live from a demonstration or product launch, take advantage of a celebrity in your premises and more. The main players are **Facebook, Periscope, Meerkat, YouTube** and **Livestream.** Unfortunately, some of the features on these platforms are completely restricted to desktop applications and others, whilst having excellent mobile apps have limited social communities to engage your audience.

For this reason, I recommend the new kid on the block, but soon to be the biggest kid on the block, Facebook's live streaming feature. The first thing to understand about live video is that you are powerful, you now have access to a live broadcast studio. Like the 6 O'Clock news, you can schedule events, have regular slots where you interact live with your community.

The live broadcast gives you access to a chat bar or messenger style app overplayed on your screen to engage and answer any questions from your fans, customers or group, in a live environment. After the live feed has finished, the video is made available on your page as a standard video, with all live chat rendered as comments.

Plan, Capture, Edit, Distribute and Track.

Worked Examples.

Demonstration

The people have amassed to show the government that democracy is powered by the people, for the people. During the event, a collection of speakers and live music is scheduled. Broadcasting live from the event allows anyone not able to attend to watch it live and interact with the event in real time. If the mainstream won't cover the event then the people will!!

Product Seminar

After a successful launch of your new product, feedback finds that customers are finding a few of the advanced features needing clarified. You set up a Facebook event and advertise it widely to your community, sending each of your Facebook members an invite. You extend the invite via your email list (assuming you collected all your customer's emails at the time of purchase) from your favourite email app. During the live presentation, you take live questions and give real time answers, both via the chat function, verbally and via physical demonstration. Your customers will love the fact that you answer their questions, respond to their calls and again you will strengthen their loyalty to your brand.

For this, you would need a camera operator and a presenter, and a second page administrator (explained in the Facebook section) on a separate phone to answer any questions via the chat function.

Cooking Master Class

Every Monday at 6PM, customers have the option to tune into a live master class from the middle of the bustling Big Eat Cafe. Prior to the Monday broadcast, the Big Eat Cafe releases the dish and ingredients needed, giving fans the opportunity to cook along at home. The chef and camera operator have a standardised plan of action for their live broadcasts. The chef introduces the dish, the ingredients, then preps and cooks the dish. The camera operator films using the phones rear camera, allowing them to keep in touch with the live questions from the fans. The camera operator selects the best questions and relays them to the chef verbally, who answers them live. The broadcast happens every week to build Big Eat's reputation.

For this you would need a camera operator and a presenter.

Treatment

Outline your entire treatment for the planned project and update it as your plan comes together.

Plan

Unlike capturing media that you can later edit before distributing, a live broadcast is just that, LIVE. Yes, you are broadcasting to the world LIVE. There are no second takes, no edits and no forgiveness, well most of the time. Everyone has seen the weather and news channel out takes. Plan and rehearse beforehand to do your best not to join them. As it is live and you don't get second chances, be very clear about what you are broadcasting. Treat it like a presentation in front of a room full of people, do your research, know your products and have your content well practised and rehearsed. The more you broadcast, the more comfortable and natural you will become presenting in front of the camera.

Theme

When filming live, always have a clear theme or objective behind the live presentation. It may be to provide unparalleled customer service or to show a particular product feature, or to demonstrate how to cook in a particular style. What ever it is, having this underlying theme or objective will help you pull yourself back on track if you begin to waffle or your mind goes blank. Define clearly your objective for the presentation before hand.

Let People know

Just like any other live event, you have to promote it before hand to make sure people attend. Broadcasting live spontaneously is not going to bring the numbers in, at least not at the beginning. You must first promote it far and wide, using all of your social media channels. Use everything at your disposal to promote the event. Stamp images with the date and time, if it is a regular show, make people aware that it will be happening daily, weekly, monthly etc. Add your Facebook page address to all media to make sure people know where to access the broadcast. But remember, no "click bate" titles, be clear about the content you are broadcasting and keep it relevant.

Time Zones

Plan for differences in time zones. If your main customer base or engagement comes from across the Atlantic, be sure to list the broadcast times in their standard time as well as local time. Make the broadcast as simple as possible to access, i.e. within your Facebook event have a link to the page, detail that this is where the Live streams occur. Stamp your Facebook page URL or key search terms onto promotional graphics, images or even create a short video to communicate how people can easily access your page. Make it fool proof and everyone will be able to find and access your live streams.

Actor

Most professional live broadcasts pay an actor, or a presenter to perform. If live is not your thing, maybe there is someone in your office or a family member that has the aspiring ambition to be the company face or prospective news anchor? This is perfect training for their future, get them onboard and utilise their passion and ambition to drive your brand.

Capture

IOS and Android

Apps

- *Facebook Pages manager. A free app that allows you to manage your pages and to live stream from them.*

Broadcasting

Access the Facebook Pages manager app and select the icon for a new post, then select the **"Go Live"** as your new post. You will be asked to give a title to your broadcast and select the camera, then you hit the

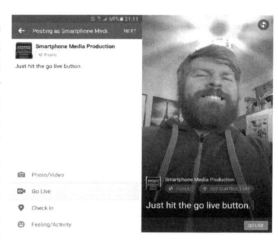

'GO LIVE' button and it will give you a count down before broadcasting live.

Portrait Mode

Currently the live broadcast from Facebook is filmed in the not so standard 'Square box' ratio. This is mainly to save on data bandwidth in the transmission, as well as providing space on screen for the live chat feature. Facebook have geared up their live service to be filmed with the handset in portrait mode, i.e. your phone is held upright, as normal. If you rotate it to the side and record in landscape mode, it wont make any difference as the ratio is a square, however if your audience is accessing it live on their mobile, the auto rotate function on their phones will always force the video onto its side, making their experience unwatchable. For viewers on a laptop or smart TV, the image will be on its side i.e. rotated 90 degrees.

Flight Mode
The advice given for recording all other forms of media does not apply for live video, as the phone needs the a network, be it 3G, 4G or WIFI in order to broadcast. However, I would recommend placing the phone on silent, so incoming emails, phone calls, messages etc do not beep and interfere with the broadcast.

Still As possible
If you have read this book cover to cover and have been blown away by the incredible amount of awesome information presented, just remember that if you pass the phone to a friend or colleague to become your live camera operator for the broadcast, they may not have read the book and may automatically go into shaky movement mode. The last thing you want is a live broadcast of you telling the operator to stand still. Convey your clear instruction to them before hand, better still buy them a copy of the book.

Smooth Movement
You may be required to move for the broadcast (close ups of

a product etc)and this must be executed smoothly. There are steady cams and gimbals for your phone these are by far the best option to ensure steady jitter free movement. Make sure it can accommodate a phone in portrait, most are only suited for mounting the phone in landscape i.e. for traditional filming)

The cheapest way to achieve steady movement is simply by being aware of your movement, this will have a tremendous effect on reducing your movement, therefore reducing any shakiness being transferred to the footage produced. Camera operators need to be able to focus and concentrate, they are as important as the presenter. Make sure they are fed and watered prior to filming to help their concentration.

Audio

Capturing audio for a live broadcast is important, again make the room as quite as possible and follow all the advice set out in earlier chapters for audio and video capture. Now, if you are using a camera operator to assist in your live broadcast just remember this operator will be closer to the microphone (unless you're using a cabled external microphone or a directional external microphone), make sure your operator is aware of this and ask them to be vigilant of the microphone's position, especially if they are relaying questions to you for answering.

Cue Cards

Have a system to detect your waffle (i.e. when you begin talking about stuff that is not relevant) and get you back on track. Some cue cards, a white board with the topics to be covered, have a time piece and be aware of your timings. Pre-plan your shots and make sure you capture them all.

Selfie Framing

When doing a selfie styled live broadcast make sure you frame your self well, a medium close up i.e. from chest up to about 20cm above your head. This shot will fill the frame. Do not stand too far away and become lost in the background, as the camera may begin to focus on background items especially if there is movement there. A selfie stick (make sure your can mount in portrait before purchase)is great for this kind of shot! Also be aware of your background, check to ensure nothing unwanted is being broadcast to the world.

Relax

It can be difficult presenting information to people on stage or live online, to the world. The first thing is practice, the more you do it, the easier and more comfortable it becomes. Relax and breath, release any tension prior to filming use any technique that works for you. Finally remember that you are talking about something you are passionate about, something that has value to you, stick to the facts, stick to the script and you will be ace.

Toilet

Its live, make sure you have used the rest room before hand.

Full Auto Only

When recording live, the only option you have is camera selection. You can either choose the front, selfie camera or the rear mounted, main camera. The rest of the options available to you when capturing standard video are automated by Facebook to optimise the compression for streaming. Choose the selfie camera if you are self operating, this allows you to see the live chat and if needed, switch the cameras. Choose the rear main camera if you are using an operator for filming. The operator then can frame using the screen as well as being able to see the chat/questions etc.

Lens
Look at the lens, not the screen and not the camera operator. Practice recording short videos (you don't even have to record), where you present to the lens. When you are looking directly into the lens, you are making eye contact with the customer or fan that is engaging with the video, it is much more personal.

Countdown
After Facebook live gives you its countdown, give your self another 3 second silent count down then take a deep breath and go. This is also a good time to get your branding in.

Monitor
On Facebook live, if you are filming a selfie broadcast you can monitor the viewer numbers, their comments and reactions. Monitor this information and react appropriately, eg **"Excellent we have just passed the 5000 live viewer mark, thank you, much appreciated. You guys are awesome."**

Branding
Unlike edited media, you will not be able to stamp your media with your company's logo. However, if you start your broadcast by filming a steady shot of a company branded poster, screen saver, mouse mat etc, this will start your broadcast off with your identity. Alternatively if you have a branded T-shirt or jumper you could wear this when broadcasting.

Title
Introduce yourself, the title and topic of the live broadcast.

If you see a large jump in new viewers then take a second to thank them and reiterate the title and topic. These folks may have just tuned in because a friend had been commenting or a friend had shared or tagged them, let them know why they are here and why they should stick around.

Live and Replay

The video will be live but as soon as you finish recording it will be available as a replay, just like any other video on your timeline. So, always remember to address both your live and replay audience.

Sharing

Encourage your live audience to share both the live and replay. Live audience can add a friend to the broadcast by clicking the plus sign on the bottom left and adding their name or by writing their name in the comment and selecting them.

Subscribe

Encourage your live audience to subscribe or "LIKE" your page so they don't miss another awesome broadcast.

Gratitude and Acknowledgement

Give "shout outs" and acknowledge your audience, they have given their time to tune in, just a short random name blast or a general thanks, makes the audience feel more of a participant than just a random viewer.

Energy

You bring the energy as the broadcast will live and die on the energy you bring to the table. Big breaths, positive vibes, smiles and at a minimum, look as if your enjoying yourself. Instil the broadcast with a raw and infectious energy that inspires others to tag and share.

Things to note

1. Age appropriate
It will be broadcast live, be aware of your audience age with regards to language and content.

2. Kill background apps
Kill all background apps to make sure your live stream is getting your phone's full attention.

3. Communication
Have some predefined way of communicating non verbally between operator and presenter, hand signs for speed up, time running out, battery running out, a reminder to mention etc. A simple method is a white board that the operator can write large simple messages on.

4. Battery
Set a time limit for your Q and A's, so you don't run out of battery as the momentum starts to build.

5. WIFI / Data
Live streaming requires data to be sent, that data is either coming from your data plan or through a local WIFI spot. The bandwidth of the data available i.e.strength of your signal connection may affect the quality of the video and audio broadcast. So be sure to broadcast from somewhere you have a strong signal.

6. Second operator
If the camera operator is replying and filming, the camera will

move as they type on the phones screen. A second operator, who is also an admin on the Facebook page could answer the questions from their own smartphone, whilst the broadcast is live. Alternatively, clearly state that all questions submitted are greatly received and will be answered shortly after the broadcast is finished.

Next level Solutions
The next level solutions are covered in a combination of the audio, photography and video solutions. The main solutions for live streaming are a microphone for audio quality and a tripod (tilt head) and/or phone mount for a steady shot.

Editing
Its live -there is no editing available via the service. However, you can use a video download service to download the video and edit it in phone before re-uploading your edit of the event, stamped with your brand etc. But this is a bit excessive.

Second operator
As mentioned earlier, a second or third operator logged into the Facebook pages app on their own phone can then begin to answer any questions that are not being answered live. Remember, everything is about service and making your customers/fan base feel included, as if they are a part of a family. Spending time to interact and engage in the comments, even after the broadcast is finished is a very wise move, that will pay off.

Distribution
You have already done the work to get a live audience to the stream. Afterwards, distribute as you would with your other videos.

Building a live audience takes time, ask any band, comedian, live act. Build it up, don't be put off by initial low numbers.

Looks at the phone's key features for communication and distribution, delving into the key social media apps of Facebook, Twitter and YouTube.

Communications

Voice Calls

APPS - Native app, Skype, Facebook, Facetime

The main key feature a phone is known for is the voice call. Most smartphone owners will have some sort of price plan that will include an allotted number of minutes for voice calling each month. However, with advancements in data compressions there are now lots of options allowing you to make phone calls via your phones data connection. Either using 3G, 4G , LTE or WIFI to connect to services like Skype, or Facebook Voice call etc. As most of these services are free, this could be a way to reduce bills whilst being productive.

Video Calls

APPS -Skype, Facetime, Hangout, Facebook

Voice calls operate over the same data systems as previously described, except this time they transmit and receive video as well as audio and therefore take up more bandwidth and more data. Each of the services offer the same base functionality, i.e. the ability to call whilst seeing your caller in a small 'picture in picture' insert on screen. However each brings something different. Google's "Hangout" is one of a few that allow conference like calls between many individuals.

Messaging service

APPS - Native Text, Whats App, Google Messenger, Facebook Messenger, I messages.

The standard text message functionality is available within every phone and like call minutes, the amount you can send over a set time period is usually tied to your price plan. However, there are many alternatives that can take advantage of the phone's data plan to transmit and receive messages. Again, be aware of your data usage in relation to your data plan, especially if you plan to send video content regularly via these messaging apps over 3/4G. Whats App and Facebook messenger are my two favourite messaging apps, mainly for the attachment options and the group messaging features. More on Facebook messenger later.

Email

APPS - Gmail, Outlook, Apple Mail

Email is a key feature of any smartphone and a core tool for any activist, organiser or entrepreneur. There is always a native way of receiving your email in every operating system, however the main three email clients have their own dedicated apps, which make available the unique features associated with their email experience directly on your mobile phone. Outlook is a powerful email client that can bring in all of your emails from across your varying work and personal accounts. You can sign up and create multiple new emails using these services. This can be handy for creating different social media accounts for specific business ventures or groups. Just be sure to take note of your email addresses and passwords.

Key Phone Features

Security

Finger print sensor, pattern lock or keycode, whichever security function you choose, the important thing is to use one. Now that you are using your phone for more and more, you want to make sure that it is secure and only you in any eventuality are able to access it.

Remote access and wipe

Both IOS and Android have features to lock down your phone and remotely wipe your phone in case it is lost or stolen. IOS can be be done via www.icloud.com/#find , simply enter your Apple ID and Password and follow the steps. Android can be be done via android.com/devicemanager , simply enter your gmail associated with the phone and password and follow the steps.

File Manager

This is another key app that comes with most phones. Some third party file browsers have extra functionality and can be downloaded from your app store. File managers are great for renaming files, sorting files into folders, moving files to different locations etc. For example, this can be very handy after you edit a few photos, to move them to a new folder, renaming them and moving them to a new folder makes it easier to identify & access the edited pictures.

Calender

A great app that is under utilised by today's phone users. Native calender apps can be upgraded with third party apps from the app store. Functionality like appointments, tasks reminders, colour coding appointments, to do lists, integrating appointments with Google maps and more. You can also run multiple calenders or diaries under different user names or emails and sync them up across cloud accounts. i.e. using a Gmail account, you can enter the details on the phone and sync that data so you can later access it on your home PC via the chrome browser. You can even embed and sync google calendars into your website. Any updates made on your phone would then automatically update on your website. Each separate email account has its own calendar.

Web Browsers
Chrome, Firefox, Opera
One of the most used features on any Smartphone is the web browser, be it to look for an event, information, find answers etc. I personally use two separate browsers, one for business searches and one for personal searches. Each of the main browsers perform the basic functionality of a web browser excellently, each brings its own layout and unique features, like bookmarks, gestures, VPN and anonymous browsing. One of my favourite features is found on the Firefox browser. Firefox allows YouTube to continue streaming, even when the phones screen is switched off, the official YouTube app as well as all the other mobile browsers close the stream when the screen turns off. Having the screen off is good for saving the battery, it also allows you to use YouTube as a music and podcast service.

Banking
Internet banking is an excellent way to keep track of your personal and business finances, now that it can be securely accessed via your bank's app. This is another good reason for having a good security password, finger print lock and access

to remote wipe for your phone.

Time/Alarms

As standard, the clock functionality comes with world time, countdown clocks and a stopwatch, as well as multiple alarms that can be set with varying ring tones, snooze settings etc. Never be late for a meeting again.

Calculator

Knowing your numbers is key to good organisation. The calculator that comes with the phone is as standard. Extra features of a scientific calculator with graph functionality etc can be downloaded from the app stores. The perfect engineer's companion.

Media Gallery

Now that you are creating media content, a good media gallery is key. The native media gallery that comes with your phone is usually shaped by the manufacturer. I like a media gallery that updates when I am changing file names and folders in my File manager App. There are many options available, I like the **"Gallery"** App.

Settings

Get to know your settings menus, I know it's rather tedious but it is key, especially now that you will be using your phone more. It is good to tweak screen settings, time out settings, battery options, battery usage, keyboard options, sync options (for emails, photos, calenders etc), un-installing apps, storage options, notifications settings, security settings, backup settings, adding new accounts, checking for software updates and more. Get in, get familiar and get tweaking.

User Interface (UI) - Skins

The user interface is the way you interact with the phone. Android has a whole world of customisation here, IOS does not have as much. In android you can download lots of apps to skin your phone (customise the look of your phone's software). These are called launchers. I use **Nova Launcher** as it allows for excellent customisation, which I use to create a fairly minimal (uncluttered) experience. You can get launchers to replicate IOS and even Windows phones, like environments and UIs.

Podcast App

I would be lost without my Podcasts. A podcast is essentially a radio show on any subject of your choosing. There are many apps available for both IOS and Android, each allowing you to search for your podcast of choice, subscribe to the artist, stream their shows and download their episodes for offline listening (offline listening allows you to listen to the Podcast on the go, without using mobile data if you're out and about.) I use my home wifi to download my weekly podcasts so I am not using my data when out and about.

PDF reader

A PDF reader is a must! Many official documents are now being transmitted as PDFs. There are many apps ready for the challenge from Microsoft "Word" like apps to book readers. My app of choice is **Amazons kindle app**, it renders the PDFs quickly and allows for easy 'pinch' zooming.

Office Application

A mobile version of **Microsoft Word** is available on both platforms but there are many alternatives, like **Google Docs** and **Google Sheets**. Keep your business documents in the

131

cloud and you can access all your key files anywhere you have a data connection.

Website Apps

If you have a wordpress (a website management and building tool) or any other website provider that has a corresponding app, you can update your website from the app, adding your new images, video and audio straight to your website from your phone. Alternatively, you can   log into your website via the web browser set to 'desktop'.

Cloud Storage

Cloud storage is essentially an extra hard drive/storage space that is hosted externally (in a large data centre), you access this storage just as you would your phones SD card or internal memory, the only difference is you need an internet connection to access your cloud storage.

There are lots of options here from Mega upload to Google Drive, Drop Box, Icloud and One drive. If you already have a Gmail (Google), Apple or Live email (Microsoft) then you already have cloud storage!! Google's drive comes free with your Gmail and gives you 15 GB of cloud storage. One drive, which comes free with a Microsoft email includes 5 GB of free cloud storage. These are automatically set up and ready to use. IOS (Apple) users get 5GB of Icloud storage, as standard.

Social Media

Choosing a Social Media network

As mentioned before, you have an entire broadcast studio in your pocket. The phone's hardware and software combined with your creativity will create excellent products to market your business, group, ideology etc. Social media platforms are your distribution network. These are the places where you are going to post your created media, ideas, products, services etc. There are hundreds of social media networks, from all encompassing sites like Facebook to professional orientated networks like Linkedin to Video specific networks like YouTube, but these are not the only networks out there. There are sites that will pay you for creating / sharing content, others are open source and don't sell your user data. There is a social network to fit your professional outlook, media platform, ethical, political or religious persuasion etc

The key thing to social media networking is to find the main network that your client base is using. If you are going to be uploading daily photos to highlight the great food being sold at your restaurant then you want to be using Instagram or Facebook, two sights that have excellent photo tagging, photo sharing and communities highly engaged in the visual elements. Like wise if you're making audio commentary for a daily politics show your best option would be to use Sound Cloud as your main network and sharing this out to a Facebook page would be the best route.

Below is a table with the most visited websites, most downloaded apps and most used apps. The most used apps are inherently from Facebook, Google and Apple. Most of these key apps come preloaded onto the handset at purchase. Games are not the most used apps. The most used are productivity, communication or social apps. As you can see Facebook, YouTube, FB Messenger are the key apps you really need to master.

1)MOST POPULAR SOCIAL WEBSITES ESTIMATED UNIQUE MONTHLY VISITORS(MILLIONS) AUGUST 2016	2) MOST DOWNLOADED APPS TOTAL DOWNLOADS (MILLIONS) JAN- JUNE 2016	3)MOST USED APPS AVERAGE MONTHLY ACTIVE USERS (MILLIONS), JAN- JUNE 2016
FACEBOOK – 1100	MESSENGER 59.7	FACEBOOK 136.3
YOUTUBE - 100	SNAPCHAT 54.5	YOUTUBE 134.8
TWITTER - 310	FACEBOOK 45.8	MESSENGER 120.4
LINKEDIN - 255	INSTAGRAM 40.4	GOOGLE MAPS
PINTREST - 250	COLOR SWITCH 39	105.7
GOOGLE PLUS - 120	PANDORA 27.3	PLAY STORE 93.4
TUMBLR - 110	YOUTUBE 22.9	GOOGLE SEARCH
INSTAGRAM - 100	NETFLIC 21.3	91.7
REDDIT - 85	SPOTIFY 21.1	CHROME 91.4
VK - 80	SLITHER.IO 19.3	GMAIL 91.2
FLICKR - 65	PIANO TILES 18.7	INSTAGRAM 88.4
VINE 42	WHATSAPP 18.6	SAFARI 83.0
MEETUP 40	STACK 17.3	APP STORE 81.7
ASK.FM 37	CANDY CRUSH JELLY	APPLE MUSIC 66.6
CLASSMATES - 15	SAGA 16.5	SNAPCHAT 61.5
	MUSICAL.LY 16.5	PANDORA 50.3
	PINTREST 16.1	GOOGLE DRIVE 46.4
	UBER 16	NETFLIX 35.6
	ITUNES U 15.1	TWITTER 35.1
	YOUTUBE MUSIC 14.4	PINTREST 34.5
	CLASH OF CLANS 13.6	SPOTIFY 31.5
	AMAZON 13.5	AMAZON 29.6
	KIK 13.1	KIK 26.9
	GOOGLE PHOTOS 12.1	THE WEATHER
	SOUNDCLOUD 11.4	CHANNEL 25.8
	GOOGLE MAPS 11.2	GOOGLE PLAY
	WISH 10.8	MUSIC 23.8
	TWITTER 10.7	GOOGLE DOCS 23.5
	SUBWAY SURFERS	WHATSAPP 22.7
	10.5	SKYPE 21.7
	SKYPE 10.2	360 SECURITY 20.3
	SUPER - BRIGHT LED	MUSICAL.LY 19.8
	9.7	GOOGLE HANG-OUTS 19.3
		YAHOO! MAIL 18.3

Basic access

Most social media channels can be accessed through your phone's browser, just as you do at home on your PC or laptop. However the key way to access your preferred social media accounts is through the official app which can be downloaded from your app store. Each of the major players have an app, some social media platforms even allow you to manage multiple accounts easily from their app (YouTube, Instagram, Snapchat, Twitter, FB Pages Manager). Updating your social media via your mobile browser can be a good way of being logged into multiple accounts at one time, e.g Facebook personal account and a Facebook business account. Your chrome browser could be logged into your personal account and either Firefox browser or the Facebook app could be logged into your business account at the same time. So you can access multiple accounts simultaneously without logging in and out all the time.

The other thing to note when surfing the web via your phone's mobile browser is the feature to 'view as a desktop', most websites will automatically resize (most websites are now built to be responsive to the size of the display screen) or it will represent as a dedicated mobile site, which in most cases makes surfing the web on your phone easier and more user friendly. However, as we become power users (experienced users), we sometimes need to see the website in all it's glory and utilise the full functionality of the website. In most cases, the mobile version or the available app has limited options, in these cases you can select 'view as desktop' via the settings in your mobile browser to experience the site as if you were on a laptop or desktop.

The Future is mobile

The stats clearly show that there are more people using Twitter via a traditional browser than via the mobile app. Whereas, those built more for mobile social networks like Snapchat and Instagram are far more popular on mobile. Snapchat has double the amount of active monthly mobile users and Instagram has triple that of Twitters. Snapchat is also the second most downloaded app for the chosen time period, which means even more active users coming soon! Twitters advantage over both Snapchat and Instagram is its huge web traction but this will change as the future of the internet becomes mobile.

"On any given day, Snapchat reaches 41% of all 18 to 34 year-olds in the United States." (4)

Early adoption

The question you must ask is "What are the kids using?", that's the social network to install and master, the youth are always two steps ahead of big business and as a small operator you can move fast and hit the trends before your competition. **Snapchat, KIK** and **Whatsapp** don't ignore these apps, download them, use them and see how you can integrate their features to promote your business.

"It is 2018, it is a phone first world" Gary Vaynerchuk (5)

Building your community

Just like building any client base or group, building your online social community takes time and effort. There will be a lot more transient visitors visiting your social media channel, some will like/subscribe and never return. The key is to build from the community you have, this will form your base. If it is a restaurant that has just opened, start by encouraging your staff to like the page and invite their friends and family to like it. Encourage all your customers to like the page in return for a one time 10% discount or simply to keep up to date with the latest offers and new menu items, encourage them to leave a review, check out new videos and upcoming promos. The key here is engagement, value and interaction. If something isn't delivering online, the alternative is always only one quick search away. As internet consumption increases, there seems to be a similar decrease in patience. Users want the information fast and if it is not delivered fast then they will go back to the search bar.

Keep people engaged by offering excellent customer service, which simply boils down to value, which is essentially your time. That is, the time to interact, comment, react and be present on your social media channels. Don't post and disappear, you have done all this work to get your creative product to get your customers attention, it doesn't make sense that when your customer reacts to it, you don't respond to them.

Evidently you will get negative comments, trolls and naysayers. Always take the internet's vast keyboard warriors with a pinch of salt and look at the positive in the situation. First off, your media is getting a reaction! So what positives are grabbing the attention of passers by? Secondly, what is their specific criticism - don't just ignore it, ask yourself 'is it valid?' and can you make improvements to it? Finally remember any criticism online is about the ideas that you have presented, not you personally! Separate the rejection of your ideas, from someone's rejection of you, redefine it and move forward. You are making your dreams, smile and keep creating.

Fresh Content

The most valuable asset you have to leverage against the competition is time. Mastering your smart phone will allow you to utilise your time more efficiently. Now you can create, update and engage your communities from anywhere with fresh content. Engagement doesn't have to be a video, or a photo, it just has to be your time!! A quick twitter update, some retweets and a few replies whilst you take the train home. It can take the form of replying to and liking users' comments generated from your earlier creative posts, as you wait for a meeting to start or it can be a full blown live stream from your latest business meeting or selecting an automated response on Facebook messenger.

Blogging

Blogging is big business, it plays an important part in getting your website, services and products indexed by Google and is great tool for the SEO (search engine optimisation) of your website. Creating fresh content for your blog should be just as important as Facebook or Twitter. Most major blogging sites like Wordpress have a mobile app which allows you to blog from your phone. Make your content worthy of being shared by your readers.

Clickbait

Clickbait is the modern phenomenon of creating a strong catchy tag line for your post that actually has little, or no relevance to the tag line. This is called clickbaiting and it will lose you fans and genuine customers rapidly.

Always populate your post with genuine content that is relevant to the catchy tag line and is of quality and value to your members, clients, customers etc. Clickbate is not how you build quality. Successful headlines or taglines are usually ones that promise time saving benefits. ie

Taglines

People want information fast, taglines tell your audience that the information enclosed is what they are looking for.

5 best ....(apps for, chicken recipes, etc)
10 best ...
Fastest way to .... (make a killer video, get 50 new customers etc)
The best .... (Facebook, Twitter, cooking) hacks

(1)http://www.ebizmba.com/articles/social-networking-websites Ebizma.com ranked 15 most popular social networks (August 2016) based on the networks Alexa Global traffic rank,as well as there U.S traffic rank from both compete and Quantcast.

(2&3)https://www.surveymonkey.com/business/intelligence/ most-popular-apps-2016/
Survey monkey takes a look at the most downloaded apps and the most used apps of 2016 (Jan - June)- All data comes from their SurveyMonkey intelligence across both Android and IOS US app

(4)Source: Nielsen Media Impact, Reach Duplication, Nielsen Total Media Fusion/GfK MRI Survey of The American Consumer 9/1/2015 – 9/30/2015 (Television, Internet, and Mobile)

(5)Dailyvee episode 080 - The stuff you don't normally see – (13:23)

Facebook

The world's NO 1 social Media platform, a place to broadcast almost everything!! Facebook can either be accessed via your phone's browser or via the native apps.

The main Facebook apps.

Facebook
Gives you access to your time line as well as almost all of the features of the browser based setup.

Facebook Messenger
A dedicated Facebook messenger app allows you to communicate with your friends and customers, create group messages, manage communications, make phone calls, video calls and more.

Facebook Pages Manager
The dedicated Facebook pages management app is an absolute must for anyone using Facebook pages. Manage all your business pages in one place, create post updates, (including live streams), view insights (analytics), reviews, check ins , calendar, schedule posts and reply to messages sent to the page with the page ID.

Facebook Groups
The dedicated groups app allows you to navigate the groups that you are a part of, and those you administrate.

Facebook Adverts Manager
A dedicated adverts manager. A must have app if you are using Facebook to advertise your products and services.

Events from Facebook
A dedicated events app to manage your business and social life. A key app if your business is social and events orientated.

Facebook Terms
Personal User Account
The standard Facebook account that represents you, populated with your photos, thoughts, passions, your likes and dislikes. This is all centred around the time-line. This account allows you to upload photos and videos, post comments, like and share other media, join and create groups, like and create pages, create events and more. Requires an email account to be set up.

Business User account
Using your business email,this is the exact same as a personal user account, in terms of features etc. This account is just a personal account, that represents your business.

Page
Pages are for businesses, organisations, charities, sports clubs, brands etc. They allow these business/groups to share their content with their customers. Their customers or "fans" need to "like" the page to see updates from the page in their personal news feed.

The Facebook user account and page are very similar in their layout and set up, the first sections here cover both, before concentrating more on the Page, as it is most relevant to business like activities.

Creating an Account
Most people will have a Facebook account already, but if you

do not all you need is a personal email account. Email accounts can be created via Gmail or Live mail. Once you have entered your email and created a password, Facebook will prompt you to enter your personal details to create a profile, then you can populate your profile with pictures, education details, likes/ dislikes and more. Once your account has been created, all of the features of Facebook are open to you.

A business account

Most people will not have a separate business account. When creating a separate account for your business, use your business email address to set it up - if you're an activist or community group and you do not have a separate email account, use a free service like live mail or Gmail to get a new email. Gmail integrates best with Google android.

A business account is a user account just like your personal account, except this is registered under your business details, still using your name. With this account, you will be able to manage all of your business contacts and pages separately from your personal account.

Creating a second user account to manage your business pages is not essential, in fact you can run all of your business pages, groups, events etc from your original/ personal Facebook account. The main reason I recommend creating a completely new Facebook profile is that you can begin to add people, send friend requests etc that are related and necessary for your business but are completely separate from your personal Facebook accounts. For example, for Robb Wallace Media I set up a new Facebook account, added local business owners, clients, equipment manufacturers, studios, actors etc. I like hundreds of pages and groups, none of which I would have added to my personal Facebook account, including those of all of my competitors. When I log into this Robb Wallace Media Facebook account, the time line is populated with relevant content from my competitors, customers, etc. Also, all updates from group discussions, events and messages are here and not integrated into my personal account. I suppose it is like creating a separate business bank account, its just easier to keep it separate.

NOTE :
If you have already created your business pages you just need to give permission to this new business account (it is seen as an individual by Facebook) to manage them, make sure you grant admin permissions to your new business account.

Setting up your business account profile
To Set up your Facebook business user profile, click on your name then go to the "About" tab. Fill in as much information that is relevant to your new business account, add your website, social media account URLs, phone numbers and contact information. If you have already created a business page you can designate your business as your place of work, if not do this after you create your business page, add a short company synopsis detailing your services or products.

Facebook tabs and Apps
There are a few tabs that most people are aware of, like "photos", "friends" and "about", but there are many more tabs and apps available. For example, if you have an active YouTube channel you can add it as a tab on your Facebook profile or Facebook page. This means your customers can access your YouTube videos directly from your Facebook page, just as easily as they can access your Facebook photos. Make things

as easy as possible for your customers.

Manage your tabs
This essentially works the same on both your Profile and your Pages. However there are more key tabs on your user profile, including 'reviews', 'video', 'photos', 'about', 'events', 'check ins', 'notes' as well as hundreds of other plug in apps like YouTube, Shopify and more. Fill in all of the relevant info that is key to your business, make it as simple as possible for the customer to find your key information, contact details, web address, opening times, street address etc.

Profile and Cover photos
The profile picture is the small image that is displayed with your posts all over Facebook, so make sure it is branded and easily identifiable at a glance. Changing your profile picture (170 x 170 pixels) and your cover photo (640 x 360 Pixels with key content not in the 50 pixels at the top or the bottom of the image.) There are many websites and apps that will allow you to create exciting profile pictures with the correct Facebook dimensions. (08/2016 – Facebook is always tweaking their dimensions)

Apps
Android
- *Cover Photo Creator*
- *CoverPro Design cover Photo*

IOS
- *Timeline Cover Photo Maker Free*
- *Facebook Cover Designer*
- *Adobe Spark*

Webistes

- *http://www.autreplanete.com/ap-social-media-image-maker*

As you will potentially have a Facebook business account and a Facebook Business Page, make sure to differentiate the Facebook User account profile picture from the page's picture. I tend to keep the user account simple, my product or my face and a cover photo stating "User Account of Robb Wallace Media".

Things to include in your profile picture page: Your logo.
Things to include in your cover photo : Your logo, tag line, products, services, a prompt and your web address,tag line, opening times, etc..

You can also add a little more distinction by adding and displaying your 'Nick Name.'

Post Privacy

When posting anything on Facebook, be it a photo, video or an event etc, the privacy of the post can be set to your preference. This allows you to post to a specific page, group or list (also called "feeds). Every post is set to either 'public' accessible to anyone and everyone, 'friends' which is accessible to all of your friends. However you can also choose to post to a specific list or feed ie family or best friends. These lists or feeds can only be created via the web browser, they can be a useful tool.

Page specifics
Creating a Page
Simply launch the Facebook app, go to settings (Top right or bottom right), scroll down to "create page" and follow the instructions. Once you have created the page, download the Facebook pages app, which is the best way to post, monitor and track your account.

Profile and Cover photos
The dimensions here are for the page to render nicely on mobile and desktop (08/2016 – Facebook is always tweaking their dimensions) – 640x 360 pixels with key content not in the 50 pixels at the top or the bottom of the image. This way the image will resize for the Desktop page and the mobile perfectly in one image. As yet no mobile apps are providing this hack.

Call to action
A central call to action button that can be configured to do many things. The options are limited but workable like, watch video, sign up, play game, use app, send message, send email, contact us, call now, book now and shop now. Press the button, then select edit to configure your call to action button.

Admins

Only Admins can assign roles to manage pages. The various roles the admin can assign have different permissions(listed below). This allows the Admin to manage the page and it's contributors. In the Pages app go to page settings, then page roles. Then click on Add person to page. Admin is the top level and has complete access to everything. I tend to give contributors 'Editor' status, as it allows them to update, upload, comment and more but gives me as the owner full power to remove them if needed.

	Admin	Editor	Moderator	Advertiser	Analyst
Manage Page roles and settings	☐				
Edit the Page and add apps	☐	☐			
Create and delete posts as the Page	☐	☐			
Send messages as the Page	☐	☐	☐		
Respond to and delete comments and posts to the Page	☐	☐	☐		
Remove and ban people from the Page	☐	☐	☐		
Create ads	☐	☐	☐	☐	
View insights	☐	☐	☐	☐	☐
See who published as the Page	☐	☐	☐	☐	☐

Posting content on your page.

When posting content that you have created or even sharing content from other pages, always tag and brand the post. As discussed within the audio, photography and video sections, make sure that your created content is branded with your logo, website, key #tags, and a prompt to like and, share as well as any further call to action. This means that when you post content to your page via the pages app and the original content is shared, when it appears on timelines throughout Facebook it will be easy for anyone looking at it to see where it came from and associate your FB page with the shared content. First impressions last.

Tagging

Tagging is the ability to link a friend, or contact into a comment, photo or video that you are posting. This is a great feature as it depends on the personal settings of the person you tag, for the post to appear on their personal timeline and therefore be seen by their friends. For most people this is what will happen but you can restrict this in settings and take control of who can tag you. For example, if you are being tagged multiple times by events that are unrelated to you.

This is where a 'business' Facebook account is extremely useful. When tagging someone you must be friends with them, you can tag pages from a page but not real people unless they have commented on one of your posts. So if I was posting a competition for Robb Wallace Media and I was posting it from my own personal account, where I do not have any of my customers, competitors or media enthusiasts as "friends", my tagging will be short lived. However If I have taken the time to create a separate account and request the friends of all my customers, competitors, industry experts, reviewers etc then I can now tag all of these folks in relevant posts, that may be of interest to them.

The other way around this is to encourage visitors to your page, posts, adverts etc to comment. Once they comment you can tag them and more importantly message them directly from your page ID, i.e. you can message them as Robb Wallace Media but they must make first contact, i.e. by commenting.

Hashtags

Hashtags are a way to search and index the search. So, if I wrote an article on health, I would hashtag **#health #fitness #wellbeing #Glasgow,** all of the key words relevant to my article. This allows me to cast a wide net of terms associated with the theme of the article, which means that if someone is searching **#fitness** for example they have a chance of finding my article.

Algorithms

Facebook uses algorithms to display relevant content on your timeline. On a daily basis you only see a small percentage of posts from the friends that you have had recent interaction with. This is different from twitter, which delivers posts in real time. Tagging a post with a name makes your account active in that person's Facebook world and therefore makes your content more likely to come up on their timeline when you post. But be aware, no one likes to get spammed!! Make your content worthy of being tagged!

If you wish to see all posts, you have to go to the settings tab

149

and click on **"most recent"** which will show you all posts from all of your friends and liked pages.

Insights

The Facebook Pages app gives you the ability to track and collect key information about your page. The app gives an overview of the page, giving you details like how many likes, new likes, total reach, post reach and people engaged. At a glance, this page is excellent and gives you the ability to see if your page is actually engaging your audience. However, if you log into your Facebook account via your phone's mobile browser set to desktop, you get full access to the insights tab, like you would if you were using a laptop. Here you get

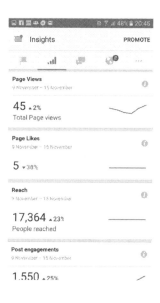

much more varied and specific detailed data. Each category is broken down with graphs, demographics and more.

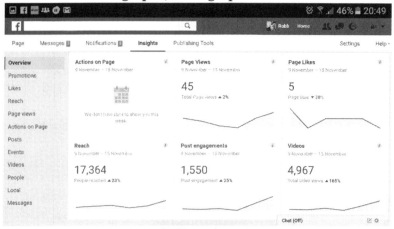

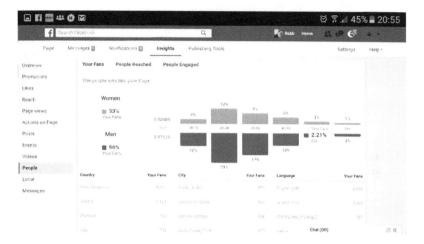

With this information you can see which demographic is engaging with your content, or with specific kinds of content, i.e. video, photos etc. You can see; what time of the day your posts are most engaging, which kind of post is most popular or which individual posts have went viral. You can see what country, age group, gender, language and more. This information is powerful and can be used to understand your audience better. Use this information as a foundation when creating content or creating a new marketing strategy. If your target audience is 25 to 45 year old males and your insights tell you its actually women 18 to 25 who are engaging with your content, then you need to look at changing it. If you're spending ten hours a week creating blogs and tagging photos and no time developing your videos but find that your videos are getting far higher engagement than your blog, then you need to re-prioritise your time and energy.

Scheduling
Within the Facebook pages app or via the mobile browser set as desktop, you can schedule your posts for the week ahead.

Simply plan all relevant content (based on your insight data) that you wish to cover in the week and set them for key times (again based on insight data.) These posts should be tagged, hash tagged etc. Scheduling allows you to have key posts at key times to engage your customers and clients, even if these times aren't suitable for you to be spending on Facebook. You can't be online all the time and scheduling is key to combat this. However, don't just schedule 100 posts for a week and wait until they run out. Yes, schedule lots of relevant posts but remember that value is the key to customer service so reply to comments and post new and relevant content over and above the already scheduled content.

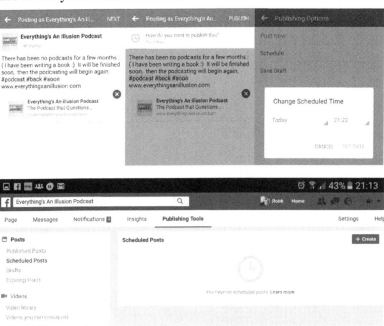

Scheduling a post can be done individually or in bulk. After writing a post for your page you are given the option to post now or schedule for a later date. If you select 'schedule', you will be given further options to select the time and date for when the post will be published. The other way is via Facebook on your mobile browser set to 'desktop', this allows you to access the publishing tools bar at the top of your page. Here, you can create multiple posts in one place and control when they are scheduled.

Auto Play videos

'Auto play' videos play automatically as you scroll down your timeline. If you have a branded intro or motion graphic as an intro then your brand will engage momentarily as potential customers or clients scroll down their personal timeline. If your video's intro is engaging enough, they may stay for the full video.

Customer service

We are social animals, we love to communicate, to gossip, to interact and it is these interactions between the customer and the page that is the key to good customers service. The reason people comment or like is to get some interaction so by providing that interaction you are providing value and it is this value that drives your social media to success.

Uploading Video

When you upload a video, you will be prompted to give it a tag line and a description, use this space to tag, hashtag, web URL and to deliver a call to action. When paying for Facebook;s video advert services you can also add a direct call to action embedded into the end of the video. This kicks in when the video finishes and the viewer is shown a button that links to your website/product etc.

Video Playlist

Video playlists have been a core function on YouTube for many years and it is now available to Facebook users. The playlist allows you to link many videos of any nature into a list. This is a valuable tool for managing your videos and sharing multiple videos at a time. For example, an adventure company could group all of it's videos by activity, creating a playlist for white water rafting, river bugs, mountain bikes etc.

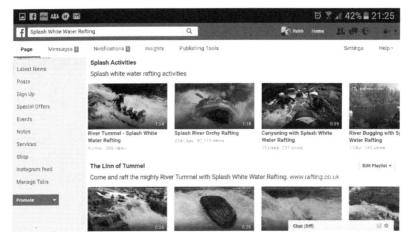

Uploading Photos

When you upload a photo or a number of photos, you will be prompted to give it a tag line and a description. Make sure your description is well tagged and has relevant links etc. You will have the option to create a single photo or a slide show. Set your browser to 'desktop' for more options (single photo ,a photo album, a slide show, a carousel and a canvas). You can add new photos to each at a later date. Creating albums is recommended to keep your photos organised and to make it easier for your customers to browser through. Creating an album called Summer 2016 or Summer Menu for example can then be easily identified, browsed and shared.

Reviews

A 'reviews' tab allows customers to leave a 1 to 5 star review on your timeline. This is a very valuable tool for receiving testimonials. However, be aware that once a review is logged, only the reviewer can edit it, so if they leave you a 1 star negative review, it has to stay. Reviews on Facebook can be shared. The tab itself can be sent via its URL (web address) to customers that have used your service. As it is easy to access and easy to use, customer uptake is good compared to a web review system. The other positive is it comes with a Facebook profile picture, and testimonials have been shown to be more powerful if accompanied with a picture. Actively target regular customers and ask them for a positive review to get the ball rolling.

Events

This feature allows you to create a calender of upcoming events. Each event listing is just a Facebook event listing, allowing you to add the address, time, specific details, add photos, invite people and more. For example, a wedding band could create an event for each gig they play, this would allow anyone of their Facebook visitors to instantly see via their events calendar what days the band are booked for and which days they still have available. An event also allows people to show interest, indicate that they are attending, invite their own friends and more. They can also subscribe to the calender to get updates about upcoming events. The details of upcoming events are listed and accessible via the page tabs. Download the stand alone Facebook Events app.

Notes

A great feature to post longer content, the note feature allows you to create a blog styled entry on Facebook. For a 'note' you add a header image, a title and then your text to the body of the note. The 'note' gives you basic text editing features not found in regular posts or comments, features like headings, quotations, bullet points, as well as allowing images to be embedded. These "notes" are a great alternative to blogging or a great place to rehash your blog material. They can also be used to create FAQs (frequently asked questions), detailed product information etc. Like a single web-page or single word document embedded in your Facebook page which can then be easily shared and organised. Allows you to create word like documents without leaving Facebook.

Visitors Posts

Depending on the settings, you can have visitor posts displayed on your 'page', on 'your post to page by visitors' and you also have the option to authorise and approve any posts before they appear on your page. Whichever way you set it up, always check your visitor posts, most of the time they are genuine customers with testimonials, questions, queries, or concerns. Customer service is key.

Sharing

Sharing content to your page is a great way to keep your audience engaged with content that fits your brand, service or product. Share relevant images, video, articles, ideas etc from other pages, as well as your own personal Facebook timeline. For example, I see a great video reviewing 'Smartphone Media Production' on a technology page I follow, I would click on the share button underneath the video. I will now be presented with three options; 'share post now', 'write post' or 'send as message'. To share the video to my page's timeline (i.e. Smartphone Media Production's page), I would select option two, 'write post'. I then see the link that I am sharing and I now have the option to add some text i.e. "What an excellent review by .... Please watch, like and share". For me to then post this to my page, as my page I need to click on 'share to Facebook' at the top of the screen. This now gives me the options to share to 'Facebook', 'on a friends timeline', 'in a group' or 'on your page', select 'on your page'. Now I am presented with a list of the pages I manage, I simply scroll down the pages and select the SMP page and and finally hit publish. This will share the content to my SMP timeline and the content will appear shared by the page and not as my personal ID. It may sound complicated but it will make more sense after doing it once.

Facebook Messenger
Facebook Messenger can be used as a stand alone app. At the moment the stand alone messenger app only allows you to access your personal Facebook friends and messages. It allows you to call, video call, organise and message, as well as a whole host of add on functionality. The power of Facebook's messenger service comes in to play when we begin to utilise it for business. At the moment the best way to access this is through the phone's browser or through the Page manager app but soon you will be able to access all of your inboxes through the messanger app. Accessing your page messages through the page manger app allows you to reply to messages, add labels to group messages of similar content or enquiry, add

notes to individual customers and reply with saved, template replies. This is the third most used mobile app, it's powerful and worth learning because its functionality and relevance for business will only grow.

Labels

Adding labels is a great way to keep your Facebook messenger organised. The label is like a folder, you can group many messages under the same label. For example, a restaurant that is getting a lot of table enquiries could label incoming messages by date, allowing any FB admin to see which customers need to be contacted, as the date arrives.

To add a label, click on messages (via page manager app), click on an individual message. Then click on the info sign next to the customer's name, then add a label. Once made, the label name can not be changed but as this is relatively new (Oct 2016) this should be remedied in upcoming versions.

Notes

The Admin note is pinned to the conversation with the aim of helping you to keep better track of the conversation but it can be used in any way you see fit. Click on messages, click on a message, to add a note click on the info sign next to the customers name, then scroll down and add a note.

Saved Replies

You can also create 'saved replies'. Create a number of pre

determined answers for your most common enquiries and save them as a draft. When standard queries come in you simply select the 'saved replies' button and select the appropriate reply. This can be extremely useful when you're on a tight deadline, you're in a meeting, at your evening meal etc.

Currently Away

Setting your status to 'currently away' means that un answered messages won't count towards your response time and rating. Something that Facebook monitors closely. It also gives your customers a better expectation of when they should expect to receive a reply.

Likes

If anyone 'likes' your page you can assign a label and a note to them by simply clicking their picture from inside the Pages app. As described above, this is fantastic for organising the interactions between your page and it's users. A powerful first step into customer management.

Facebook Messenger's open rate is far superior to email, more and more customers are using messenger to interact with companies. The customer can see if their message has been read and can see if someone is currently replying etc . Messenger is the future of small business, start learning now to manage your FB Messenger/Page messenger account and as the features released by Facebook develop you will be ready to integrate them into your business. As Messenger develops as a platform, one of its most likely evolutions will be a fully integrated Customer Management System. In the future, your business will handle sales transactions within Messenger and everything will be accessible via your phone.

Twitter

Twitter is one of the main social media platforms, it has a huge following, with millions of active users, mainly due to its corporate uptake. One of the key differences between Twitter and other platforms is the restriction on character allowance. With Twitter, your tweets are limited to 140 characters.

The other main difference between Twitter and Facebook is that tweets are not algorithmic based(Maths), i.e. you only see the tweets that are happening when you are logged on. To see older tweets, you need to scroll down your timeline. Facebook, on the other hand uses algorithms to give weight to popular posts. When you log in, your timeline displays the posts that Facebook thinks will be most relevant for you. These post are collected from the time of your last log in. However, in the future, Twitter may change over to an algorithm based timeline.

A lot of celebrities, government officials and corporate leaders use Twitter and are personally responsible for their own accounts, whereas YouTube or Facebook page accounts will usually be managed by a worker specifically employed to manage the social media account. Twitter accounts are a good way to interact and spread your brand directly to some of the key people in your industry.

Twitter account

Use your business email to create an account and pick a unique twitter user name. For example **@pro_smartphone** = Smartphone Media Production **@R_W_Media** = Robb Wallace Media, **@MMA_show** = The MMA Show. Maximum

160

15 characters but ideally make it as short as possible. The shorter your name, the better it is for others replying and re tweeting. Twitter user names count towards your 140 characters when you reply to tweets. Try your best to match your user name to your brand.

Profile Picture

Choose an image like your logo, brand ambassador etc something that identifies your product, brand, service or identity. Use the same images as your other social media channels. Dimensions for the perfect picture is 400 x 400 pixels. This is what most people will see first, this is a great place to put key information, website, products and services.

Apps
Android
- *Collage Flow*

IOS
- *Cover image, Adobe Spark*

Browser
- *http://www.autreplanete. com/ap-social-media-image- maker/#twitter*

Short description

Again, your restricted to 140 characters but you know your business so that's not a problem. This is the first thing someone will read, after your cover image if they land on your profile. Make it relevant. Pin a tweet to your profile to add an extra 140 characters and an image to your profile description.

Location
List your location.

Website
List your website or primary social media channel.

Follow me

Twitter is set up with "Follower" and "Following". At a glance, you can see how popular your account or any other account is. The most popular accounts will usually have a high ratio of followers to following. For example, a popular account could have 1.5 M Followers to them Following only 45.

Following
These are the people you choose to follow, make them relevant to your product or service. Almost everyone and everything is on Twitter. Search for specifics i.e. an individual, a company, a person or search for folk who have mentioned your key words in their tweets. There are many services available online that will allow for mass following, keyword search with auto follow and more to allow you to bulk automate this process.

Followers
Followers are simply those who have chosen to follow you. Everyday, your followers will grow, most will be folk of a similar theme as your self, some will find you by searching keywords relevant to them, some by the retweets and replies, others still from automated bulk follow software. Be aware that there are a lot of spammers and scammers, so definitely filter (be selective) of the accounts you "Follow back". Follow back is a trend where you follow back anyone who follows you. I tend not to do this and only follow back anyone relevant to my channel, I don't want irrelevant garbage on my timeline.

Lists

Lists are just that, lists of people that you follow. You can name your list and add all relevant people into that list, then when you access the list, it just appears like your timeline but only with those select accounts from the list. Lists are good to manage who you are following as your twitter account grows. Create lists for customers, influencers, competitors, important people etc.

To create a new list, tap on the home tab, then tap on lists and then the + sign. Create your new list. Now you're ready to go. Now search for those you wish to add, navigate to their profile and tap on the further settings icon and add them to your list of choice.

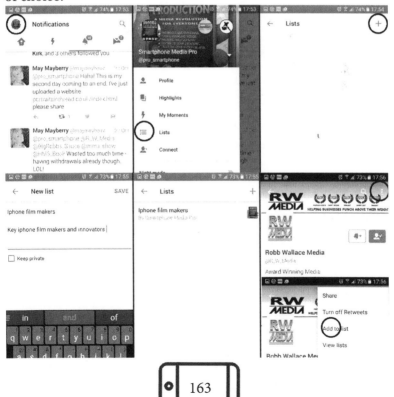

Individual notifications

You can favourite an individual account by going to their profile and tapping on the notification icon. You are then notified anytime they tweet. This can be very useful if there is a big industry announcement you don't want to miss or for key people you don't want to miss updates from.

Tweeting

Tweets

The primary aspect of Twitter is the "Tweet", 140 characters long. That is 140 characters to address your audience or anyone you are replying to. Twitter no longer shortens your 140 characters by 22 characters for adding a URL, photo or video. However using only 140 characters to express yourself is a skill. The discipline of only having 140 characters to use is good for getting to the core of what you are actually trying to say. Cut back the waffle, take out the dead wood and get straight to the point.

Images and Video

When adding an image, Twitter will take you to it's general media browser, a simple display that categorises all of your images in order of age, newest first. If the image you wish to upload is a recent image then just scroll down a little and click on it, however if you have been creating images and storing them in folders, categorising and preparing them, as mentioned earlier then you need to press the image gallery button. This will now take you to your primary image browser where you can search through your media folders and select the image.

Video

You can attach videos to your tweet. The current limits are

512MB or 30 seconds. You can also upload a video that you record at the time of tweeting via the Twitter app. To do this, simply click on the camera icon, you will then get the option to take a picture or make a video, click and hold the video icon to record a single clip or multiple video clips totalling up to 30 seconds for direct upload to twitter. If you take multiple videos, there is a very simple timeline editing option available within Twitter's video upload option. For example, if you take five short videos totalling thirty seconds, they will all be on an editing timeline and you can re-arrange their order of play. Just like the limited characters of a tweet, this style of video (i.e. short - 30 seconds max) will force you to be creative, no lazy shots, you must make every shot count.

Reply

You can reply to anyone's tweet by pressing the reply symbol. When replying, everyone involved in the original message username will appear. This eats into your character allotment, so if you only want to reply to the original sender, delete all of the others. If you just write your reply and press send, this will be seen as a direct reply and it is only sent to those usernames in the body of the tweet. If you put text (recommended) or a simple period symbol ".", before the username of the intended recipient, or as the first character of the tweet before their username, the tweet will be sent to those you are replying to, as well as all of your followers. Both options have their advantages.

Retweet

This is your way of re-broadcasting any tweet that you enjoyed. Re-tweeting is a good way to get others to retweet your tweets. Only retweet or endorse content that strengthens your brand etc, don't just retweet for the sake of it. As they come up on your timeline, make sure that the content you retweet is relevant, in theme with your brand and with what your "followers" would expect from your channel.

Favourite
'Favouring' a tweet is the equivalent of "liking" a post on Facebook. To favourite, click on the heart symbol.

Tweet Activity
From your profile page, you can click on the small graphic icon to see your tweet activity. Here, it will give you a very general impression number, which is the number of people who have seen the tweet. Total engagement, which is the times people have interacted with the tweet i.e. replied, watched the attached video etc. Media Engagement, this tells you how many times your media has been clicked. These tools give you a basic overview of how people are interacting with your tweets.

YouTube

The last of the three main social media channels is YouTube, which is a Google product and is the market leader in hosting and streaming video. Facebook is doing wonderful things with targeted video and you should always try to upload to both platforms. However, the key advantage that YouTube has over its competitors is that it is not time restricted. Items posted on both Facebook and Twitter have a very immediate effect, with little to no searching through old posts, however YouTube is all about searching, be it to look up a product review uploaded four years ago, or to listen to a motivational business seminar uploaded five months ago etc etc. With YouTube, good content has longevity! The key parameter that Google uses to judge the success or rank of a video is engagement,– i.e. how long, as a percentage viewers stay engaged with your video, this is the key to determining the weight of your video in it's search rankings, so always cut any dead wood from videos in the edit as it will only kill your engagement.

YouTube channel
If you are only creating one YouTube channel, just sign up and create it. Your Google account (Gmail email) works across all Google products, including YouTube.

Creating a new channel
Unfortunately this can't be done via the app!! You can use the app to view, comment, browse, upload, edit, create playlists and play videos but to be able to create a channel and customise it, you need to log in via the mobile browser set to desktop or on a laptop or PC to begin.

To get started, go to YouTube via the mobile browser set to desktop or on a PC or Laptop. Sign up or login with your Gmail account and create a new channel for your brand. Creating a channel seems to continuously change, at the time of writing this, it is top right hand side to click on your avatar (profile pic), then create a new channel and follow the instructions. Google likes to change how it does things on a regular basis.

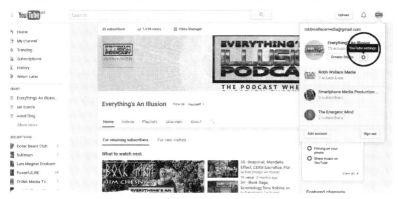

My Channel

Navigate to the settings where you can begin to customise your channel, click on the three horizontal lines on the top left hand side. This will open up a menu, click on My channel.

Header image
Websites

- *http://www.autreplanete.com/ap-social-media-image-maker/#youtube*
- *https://www.fotor.com/features/youtube.html*

The header should be in keeping with your other social media channels. YouTube has a profile badge and a header.

The profile badge is the small image that is displayed when you comment on other videos and the header is seen when someone visits your channel, via web, TV or mobile. The best dimensions are 2560 x 1440 pixels.

You can add all of your social media accounts, as well as your website to the bottom right hand side of your header image. Once added, each of these will be direct links to the respective channels. To add your social media channels, go to the top right hand side of the header image, hover your mouse over the top right and click the pencil, then click "edit links." Alternatively, you can click the "about" tab. Here, you can add a description of your activities, add an email and add links to your header image. The URL must have http:// in front of it to display the relevant icon on the header. Once added, they will display at the top left on a PC and in the "about section" in the app.

About

As with Facebook and Twitter, write a nice piece selling your expertise, position yourself in the market, show a testimonial, opening times, schedule etc. Write the information you would want to see if you had actively searched and clicked on the about link. Don't leave it blank.

Video manager

Some final things to set up in the mobile web browser set to desktop, before we can revert to the YouTube app. In "My channel", then click on the "video manager" and then on the left hand side click on "channel".

Channel

In channel you have the below options, click on the tab and fill in the details.

1. Status and Features

Verify your account, add your phone number. YouTube will then send you a code via text, type it in to complete the verification. This allows you to make money from your videos, as well as upload videos longer than 15 minutes and more.

2. Monetization

Before you can make money you have to set up an Adsense account (this is where Google will tabulate your earnings). This is a Google product and is set up with the same Gmail account. YouTube layers your videos and your channel with relevant adverts. It pays to have great content, videos that get a large number of views and great engagement command better adverts and generally make more money.

3. Upload Defaults

Here you can automate a lot of features and save yourself a lot of time and repetition.

3a. Category

Excellent if your videos are always in the same category . i.e. Sports, Comedy etc

3b. Description

Add a brief description as well as all your social media and websites, this will be added to the description of every video you upload.

3c. Tags
Create the general tags that every video will share, i.e your brand name.

3d. Save
Change any other default that you wish.
After you change any default options click "save."

4. Branding
You can add a channel brand that appears small in the corner of every video. Upload your brand image to lock your videos to your brand.

Youtube App
Changing Channels
If you set up more than one YouTube channel, you can easily change between these in the app. Click on the Person icon which will display the profile of the active account. Tap the screen under the profile badge on the left and select the account you wish to use.

Video Uploads
Once your channel is set up, you can log in via the app and upload videos. To upload a new video, click on your avatar to access your channel then click on the upload icon. This will take you to the phone's gallery, select the video you wish to upload and begin. Video eats a lot of data, if your running low on mobile data use WIFI. Give your video a catchy title, add some description, tags and set its privacy (Public = Everyone, Unlisted = anyone with the link can see it, Private = you must invite users to view the video). Then share it out over your

other networks/channels.

Playlists

Playlists are a great feature. YouTube allows you to create playlists of your own uploaded videos and from any other videos on YouTube. A new playlist requires a title and will benefit from a description as well.

Your created playlists can be set to private, unlisted or public, just like your videos.

An example of using playists could be
1- Categorising of all your relevant content into one playlist.
E.g 1- for a Video Menu - Title - Big Robb's Restaurant Video Menu - Description - All of our fantastic dishes are served daily, freshly prepared by our excellent chefs. Have a look over the video menu and see what dish you would like to order. Book your next visit now by visiting http://www.bigrobbs.co.uk

2- A heavy metal music band with a great new track is finding it hard to get views on YouTube. Using YouTube's playlist feature I would create a playlist titled 10 best metal songs EVER!! Then I would write a small description detailing the bands, one paragraph each. Within this playlist, I would add the bands new track amongst the 9 other tracks. I could also create playlists called "Best NEW UK Metal artist 2016", "10 of the Best New Metal Talent" etc etc. Mix the playlist with popular songs from some of the largest performers in the genre.

3- I use "Playlist" a lot to teach. Say you are an activist and you are looking to explain to a set of people their rights with regards to a particular topic. Using either your own videos or relevant videos from You Tube, you can create a simple playlist like the chapters in a book. Then send this one link out as an email for you audience to watch.

You can create playlists from your phone easily. When watching a video that you wish to add to a playlist, simply touch the screen, then press the plus sign on the top right of the screen and select one of your playlists to add the video to, or create a new playlist to add it to.

Subscribe
Encourage your viewers with a video message to subscribe to your channel, they will then be updated with each new video you upload but not unlisted or private listed videos.

YouTube Studio App
(Download from the app store)
This is a separate YouTube app that gives you your YouTube channels analytics. The app allows you to see comments, revenue, video discovery, audience, engagement and more. All of these are key factors about your audience and should be regularly checked to see how your videos are performing.

Non app features to consider
Unfortunately, with YouTube most key creative features are easier to access and manipulate via a PC or Laptop. After creating and uploading videos from your phone and the YouTube app, you could access YouTube via your laptop to adjust and change additional settings. Hopefully, further mobile integration will be arriving shortly. Features to check out via the laptop are.

Custom thumbnail

An image added to the video to help it stand out, all of the top YouTube users use them. The most simple thumbnail is a related image (related to the main content of your video) with the keywords for the video written boldly over the image. This allow a prospective viewer to instantly see what the video is about and can be made in most photo/graphics editing apps.

Subtitles and Captions

Adding subtitles to your videos is good for foreign language visitors, as well as adding another layer of relevant words to your video that Google will index for its search results, i.e. better SEO (Search Engine Optimisation). This can be very time consuming if you're uploading one hour seminars.

Call to action

A call to action is a way of overlaying messages and links on top of your videos. These are great if you're prompting your viewer to check out a product or service, asking for them to subscribe or check out other videos in the series.

YouTube is a very powerful platform, of which this chapter has just scratched the surface. Most videos uploaded to YouTube disappear in to the abyss, get your video out via social media and make sure your videos make an impact.

Google Plus

For some, Google is the internet! It is the power house behind the world's most popular search engine and also the Android phone system. However, Google is so much more than a search engine and a good smartphone operating system. It has created lots of platforms and lots of tools for you to maximise your interaction with it's products. It's main product or service is advertising, you must remember that Google is a business that makes money from user data and adverts. You trade your personal data for the free services.

As good as Google is at search, it has always struggled to create a social media platform to rival Facebook. It bought YouTube and made it into the largest and best video platform, but even though it's social media platforms have offered many features they have always had a poor uptake in comparison to it's other products and services. However, as Google is the major search provider, having an active Google + account is always good for your website's ranking and SEO.

App: Google Plus

The app allows you to see and manage both user profiles and business pages, browse and create collections, communities and events as well as upload video and photos. The app allows you to easily switch between multiple Gmail addresses (profiles), this part of the app is displayed in a similar fashion to Google's YouTube app.

Google +

A nice, easy to use social media platform that integrates excellently with all of Google's other features and services.

Google + allows you to do almost everything that Facebook does, post updates, photos, links, videos, create events, business pages, reviews and more. If you are planning on becoming a heavy YouTube creator, I would recommend investing some time getting to grips with Google +, as it integrates excellently with YouTube and it is key for creating multiple YouTube pages under the one user account email. To make multiple YouTube channels you need to create multiple Google Plus business pages. These pages are similar to Facebook's pages.

Google + pages
Create a business page just as you have for Facebook, fill it with your contact information, website, product info and more. This is an excellent tool for SEO (search engine optimisation), as an active Google plus account will give weight to your online presence, it is one of the many factors that Google ranks your website's relevance on. If yours is active and your competitor hasn't set one up, bonus SEO points to you. You can also create a custom URL for your pages ie **https://plus.google. com/+Robbwallacemedia** **https://plus.google. com/+Smartphonemediaproduction** using your name or keywords.

Google Reviews
Just like Facebook reviews, Google plus has a feature to allow customers to leave a review on your Google plus business page, for instance you could navigate to the above link and leave a review. This would then begin to increase your weight within Google.

Collections
This is a way to group your Google plus posts together. For

example, a restaurant could group all of their specials, offers, vouchers, deals, cocktails etc into individual collections. This makes it easy for potential customers to see what is available without aimlessly scrolling down another timeline. It also makes it easier for the restaurant to share out their etc.

Communities
This is the Google plus equivalent to a Facebook group, create them for everything and anything you want. Communities are a great place to distribute your content, but don't just sign up and drop your links then leave, spend some time communicating with others in the community, build your reputation, answer questions, integrate. This way your content will be welcomed and not avoided like the spam it would otherwise be.

Events
A simple yet effective way to add and invite friends to an event. Similar to all event apps, its simple and intuitive to use.

Google + Profile Images
Us the Autreplanete website to create perfectly sized Google + background and profile images.
- *http://www.autreplanete.com/ap-social-media-image-maker/#google*

Google's main apps for Android and IOS
Google's free apps are usually amongst the best in their category, they are always amongst the most used apps and are always a safe bet for a robust, well thought out app.

Google Drive
Google's free cloud storage solution gives you access to 15 GB of free cloud storage as well as full sweet of cloud based

productivity apps, like google docs and more.

Google drive is also a great place for transferring files, and storing excess files when your phone gets full. Google's drive is also a fantastic place to move all of your business documents to. This means you can easily access them at all times from your phone, laptop etc. I used Google's drive to sync up all the edits and re-edits of this book before publication, allowing me to access my work from one central place from any device, and at anytime.

Google Docs
Create and read various documents.

Google PDF viewer
Allows you to view PDF files.

Google Gmail
A great app for accessing Google's popular email service.

Google Chrome
Googles web browser. Very popular and very fast.

Google Calender
Great for organising your calender across multiple Gmail accounts.

Google keep
Allows you to take and organise notes.

Google messenger
Replaces the native SMS app.

Google Snapseed
Excellent photo editing app.

YouTube Creator Studio
A must have app for any serious Youtube user. Analytics for your YouTube account.

Google Adsense
Great for tracking how much money your Google adverts and YouTube videos have made.

Google Analytics
Allows you to monitor your website's data. This is a must for anyone who is managing a website, it allows you to keep track of your visitors, bounce rate, country of origin etc.

Google Earth
Satellite style views of anywhere on earth, integrates great with Google VR (Virtual Reality).

Google Maps
Google's SatNav is a must for navigating. Options include car journeys, public transport, taxis and walking.

Google goggles
A unique app that translates photos to real text. For example, you can even take a picture of a foreign road sign and this app will translate it into English!!

Google photos
A great organiser for your images.

Google Camera
Very simple, yet powerful camera app.

Google hangouts
Video calling across multiple users.

Google Duo
Simple high quality video calling.

Google Spaces
An app for collaborative ideas, that allows you to create your own "space" to discuss and share ideas with anyone you chose.

Google my business
Gets your business listed in Google's business directory.

Google Cardboard
Google's excellent virtual reality app. Allows you a glimpse into the future, it allows you to fly around Google earth in full 3D VR, take museum tours, ride roller coasters and more.

Google Translate
Translates pages, text etc between hundreds of languages.

Conclusion

Throughout this book you will have read lots of information with regards to planning, capturing, editing and distributing your content. Here is where the real journey begins, a book like this can only give you the information and point you in the right direction. The art of creating is developed from the time you commit to it, there are no short cuts! Today, you may be an expert in your field but remember that you once started at the beginning just like everyone else. Take the time to play, have fun and create, applying the information presented in this book. And there lies the key, having fun!! Creativity is about passion and that energy will translate and transmit through your creative projects. Choose a fun project to gain your experience through, i.e. if you are thinking about creating video menus for YouTube and Facebook, then make a few practice videos cooking at home first. Load them into the apps, play with the audio, video, effects etc. Get your skill levels up before you unleash your creative content to the world. But remember that the creative project, once complete is just the start, distributing it and getting it seen, starts a new journey.

The information presented with relation to media creation is pretty much timeless, however the technology and the apps that use the principles will continuously change. Aspects of Facebook, Twitter and Google changed within the time it took to write this book. There will always be updates (accessible through your app store) to the apps you use regularly as well as completely new apps to try, please try them.

Your phone is a powerhouse of broadcast potential. Now you have the knowledge of how you can put the technological marvel to use, no longer will you be a passive content consumer, you now have the potential to be an active content creator!

Finally, everything can be done on the phone, however all of the information presented, in part or in whole, will transfer over to traditional media production with cameras and PCs.

Have fun and stay awesome.
Robb

PS : Feel free to review, blog, tweet, leave a testimonial etc about the book online. Our Social Media channels can be found at www.smartphonemediaproduction.com

PPS: A short video testimonial would be cool :)

"Small minds talk about people - medium minds talk about events - great minds talk about ideas - and the best minds act on their ideas"

Bio

Robb Wallace has a BA in Broadcast Production with distinction from the University of the West Of Scotland, where he won the coveted court medal for academic excellence. He has also won the Edinburgh Mountain Film Festivals "Go Fast" People's Choice award. He has over ten years creating online content and has created numerous online brands, channels and projects.

He currently runs his own media business www. robbwallacemedia.com, when not on his phone he can be found grappling, travelling and eating.

Printed in Great Britain
by Amazon